Date Due

MAY - 4 1978		MAR 0 8 1993	
MAY 1 8 1978		MAR 2 3 1993	
JUN 2 1978		FEB 2 7 1997	
AUG 2 4 1978		MAR 2 1 2003	
SEP 1978		APR 2 6 2004	
NO			
DEC			
JA			
SEP			
APR			
MAY - 4 1978		7729	8695
JAN 1069		NOV 2 7 19	APR - 7
MAY 2			
DEC MAY 1 8 1978		2019	14958

CANADA WITHOUT QUÉBEC

John D. Harbron

Musson Book Company
A Division of General Publishing Co. Limited
Don Mills, Ontario

First published 1977 by
Musson Book Company
a division of
General Publishing Co. Limited
30 Lesmill Road
Don Mills, Ontario

First printing

Canadian Cataloguing in Publication Data

Harbron, John D., 1924-
   Canada Without Québec

Bibliography
Includes index.
ISBN 0-7737-0033-1 bd. ISBN 0-7737-1016-7 pa.

1. Canada — Politics and government — 1963-*
2. Quebec (Province) — Politics and government — 1960-
3. Quebec (Province) — History — Autonomy and independence
   movements. I. Title.

FC609.H37   971.06′4   C77-001376-7
F1034.2.H37

Hardcover ISBN 0-7737-0033-1
Quality paperback ISBN 0-7737-1016-7

Printed and bound in Canada.

TABLE OF CONTENTS

El respeto al derecho ajeno es la paz.

("Respect for the rights of others is peace.")

Benito Juárez, Zapotec Indian and four times
president of Mexico, 1861-72

PREFACE

The late American historian Dr. Herbert Eugene Bolton developed the theory of the common history of the Americas, in which he analyzed the evolution towards independence of the European colonial empires of the New World—English, Spanish and Portuguese.

This book extends the Bolton thesis to the fourth colonial empire, by projecting the shape of a future hemispheric republic of Québec.

Intellectual ideas are never completely new; they must extend and build on what went before. My acknowledgment is to Dr. Bolton, and to those of his protégés who were my professors when I was a young scholar of Latin American studies. From this basis of a hemispheric view, rather than the more familiar Canadian one, this book and its concepts of a Canada without Québec have emerged.

My profound gratitude goes to my alma mater, the University of Toronto; and to its John P. Robarts Library, which contains a complete record of the political and literary works of Québec nationalism and separatism.

My regret is that few, if any, of our national leaders from the English-Canadian culture will ever take time to make their personal acquaintance with the historic and contemporary writing of a part of our country intent on separate nationhood. At this time of profound national crisis, those who have called for a Québec nation will continue to go unread by the leaders who are trying to hold the country together with little or no knowledge of the roots of separatism.

I wish to thank a host of my fellow Canadians for their ideas, attitudes, comments, criticisms, witticisms and guidance. None of them is responsible for the direction of this book. Indeed many of them will be strongly opposed to its thesis.

My thanks to Arnold Agnew, John Bassett, George G.

9

Bell, J.L.P. Bernatchez, L.A. Bourgeois, Jack Bowen, Martha Braide, John C. Cairns, William Casselman, Jean Charpentier, Michel Chevalier, Danielle Choquette, Jacques A. Dextraze, Jean-Charles Falardeau, Lawrie Farrington, John Fisher, Philip J. Foster, Alastair Gillespie, Gérald Godin, Melville M. Goldberg, Anita Gordon, my wife Sheila, Alan Heisey, John S. Jenkins, Fraser Kelly, Robert Keyserlingk, Laurier LaPierre, Daniel Latouche, Romeo Leblanc, H. Ian Macdonald, John Thomas McDonough, Brigid Munsche, Gordon Murray, Jack C.M. Ogelsby, Geoffrey Pearson, John B. Pennefather, John Saywell, D. McCormack Smyth, John Sokol, Donald H. Thain and Pierre Elliott Trudeau.

My special thanks and personal gratitude goes to copy editor Karin Judkins for her persistence, devotion and enthusiasm in helping me polish the manuscript.

Finally, the theme for this book emerged from an essay I wrote for the December 1965 issue of the Montreal journal *Cité libre*, entitled "Québec and the emergence of Latin societies."

At the beginning of that essay I commented: "Québec's political, economic and social emergence in this decade is distinct only in the sense it is the first 'Latin emergence' in the Western Hemisphere to come from a French rather than a Spanish culture."

The concluding sentence read: "The question the new Québec technocrats must immediately ask themselves as they impatiently renew a once-backward province is, what kind of destiny are we preparing for and will we control it in the long run?"

This book has answers for these questions.

John D. Harbron
Toronto
Summer 1977

1

Denying Our Geography

1

For us, these four Americas are four great provinces
of a continent that moves along different paths in
search of the same freedom.

> Germán Arciniegas,
> Colombian philosopher
> and diplomat

Canada without Québec is now a reality. Québec can be a
new republic by the 1980s.

The long-term historical development of the Western
Hemisphere is embraced by four major European colonial
traditions: English, French, Spanish and Portuguese. Only
one of these, the French, has not been resolved in the
formation of a separate hemispheric nation.

Canadians reject historical determinism. Yet the history
of the inevitable self-determination of colonial peoples
dictates that Québec must withdraw from the Canadian
experience and form the last large Latin republic of the
Western Hemisphere.

Few of us can visualize Québec as a "Latin" republic
because we have not seen Canada as "hemispheric".

13

The Republic of Québec will be French-speaking instead of Spanish- or Portuguese-speaking, but as large as Venezuela, as rich as Brazil in natural resources, and close to Mexico in "national identity" in cultural terms.

For two centuries, Québec's historians, writers, politicians and priests have insisted on the "American" origins of their society. Other Canadians have looked to their many European homelands and have clung to Old World values. Unlike the Québécois, we English-Canadians have found few New World ones.

Québec's imminent departure poses questions we have not asked before.

Does Canada have a common history with the Americas? Has the Canadian national identity been inhibited by our reticence to identify with the Latin societies in our hemisphere?

Will Québec's going compel a smaller Canada to think at last in hemispheric terms if it is going to survive as an independent entity?

Can we learn what our future will be by analyzing our role in our own hemisphere?

What have we done so far to guarantee sovereignty protection in our Arctic, to promote techniques for national development, and to maintain control over dominant industries which are mainly foreign-owned, by countries which will put new pressures on Canada to cease our present trend towards economic nationalism?

Finally, what can a comparison of Québec with other hemispheric republics tell us about the future economic, cultural and social shape of a Québec republic?

If the fortunes of the colonial wars of the eighteenth century had worked in France's favor, one or more French republics might have emerged in the Northern Hemisphere. These might have included Louisiana, which embraced much of the Ohio Valley, the many French military and trading posts along the length of the Mississippi and its hinterlands, and of course the seminal colony of New France.

In fact, France made three attempts to build a New World empire. The first was the colony of New France; the second was the unsuccessful attempt by Napoleon III to establish a French empire in Mexico between 1864 and 1867; and the third was France's effort to build the Panama Canal in the 1880s, which if successful could have resulted in French instead of American domination of the Caribbean at the beginning of the twentieth century.

The major Spanish and Portuguese New World empires all moved to independence between 1776 and 1898. Only Spanish-speaking Puerto Rico, an appendage of the Spanish West Indies of the last century, remains a self-governing *estado asociado* ("associated state") within the United States.[1]

All of French America, with a few exceptions—the future Republic of Haiti; the islands of Martinique, Guadeloupe, St. Pierre and Miquelon; and French Guiana—was absorbed into British North America after the Treaty of Paris of 1763.

But when the English victors in the Seven Years War (1757-1763) guaranteed the preservation of the French language, the Catholic faith and the existing social structure of New France, they also assured the formation of a French state-in-being in North America.

Québec's patriots, intellectuals, historians and politicians—including many who do not believe in separation—have understood and articulated the place of Québec in America; while English-Canadians, including many of the intelligentsia, have often misunderstood or rejected such historical interpretation.

English-Canadians view Québec's secession as repugnant; as an exercise in destructive romanticism. But they have failed to comprehend that in the development of her provincial institutions of education, culture and commerce,

PORTUGAL
SPAIN

NEWFOUNDLAND
ST. PIERRE
MIQUELON

HUDSON
BAY

QUÉBEC

NEW FRANCE

ARCTIC CIRCLE

ALASKA

HUDSON'S BAY
COMPANY

NEW YORK

THE
THIRTEEN
COLONIES

SPANISH LOUISIANA

VICEROYALTY
OF
CALIFORNIA

GULF
OF
MEXICO

VICEROYALTY OF
NEW SPAIN

MEXICO
CITY

PACIFIC

ENGLISH

FRENCH

SPANISH

PORTUGUESE

In 1713, the French colonies in the western hemisphere represented one of the
four great European empires of America. The others were the British, Spanish
and Portuguese.

ATLANTIC
OCEAN

PAPAL LINE OF DEMARCATION 1494

GUADELOUPE
MARTINIQUE

CARIBBEAN SEA

BR. D. FR.
GUIANA

VICEROYALTY
OF
BRAZIL

RIO DE JANEIRO

LIMA

VICEROYALTY
OF NEW GRANADA

VICEROYALTY OF PERU

PORTUGAL
SPAIN

OCEAN

THE AMERICAS 1713

REG. HEWSON

and with the existence of both a national ideology and a national literature, Québec has long resembled the Spanish-American nation states which achieved their political independence 150 years ago.

Québec's intellectuals have struggled to give reality and meaning to this separate identity, notwithstanding Québec's participation in the many material and political benefits of Canadian Confederation and, since 1945, in the North American economic boom and increasing affluence.

The strong identification of Québec as "American" in her history, culture and institutional emergence is in the mainstream of Québec's history and in much of her political thought and literature.

Jean Bruchési, the conservative Québec historian, saw French-speaking Canadians conducting themselves "like citizens of America."[2]

A.R.M. Lower, the distinguished English-Canadian historian, sees English-Canadians identifying themselves by comparison as "citizens of the British Isles living in Canada."

An ideology of the nation state, and what I call a national literature of separation, have existed for a long time in Québec. The reactionary Catholic visionaries of the 1920s and '30s envisioned a Catholic "Laurentian Republic" on the banks of the St. Lawrence, while the separatists of the 1970s call for a socialist hemispheric republic; the theme of Québec nationalism changes only in its definition and inspiration.

The Catholic nationalists of the 1930s called for a nostalgic return to New France and popularized the motto *Notre maître, le passé* ("Our master the past"). The secular separatist of modern Québec rejects this nostalgia for the past. His path is *libération* from the "colonial structures" of Québec: the English-Canadian and foreign-owned business interests, the church and its political allies who together perpetuated the old order.

The poetry of revolution is renewed in the thoughts of today's Québec militant. From Hubert Aquin, the poet laureate of separatism killed by his own hand, come harsh revolutionary words. They are Québec's victory shouts, like the *gritos* of Castro's Cuba. "An apocryphal sacrament binds us indissolubly to the revolution," he has written. "That which we have begun, we will finish."[3]

The message is changeless; it is the call for a new state to be born where New France, the colonial predecessor, the home of an American people, had flourished.

If we want to understand the militancy of the Parti Québécois government, we must understand the intellectual commitment of both leaders and youthful rank and file to a national ideology and a separatist view of their past.

Listen to these words of René Lévesque, written in the year he began to nationalize Québec's power industry as minister of hydraulic resources in the Liberal cabinet of Premier Jean Lesage: "You are helping the men and women of today to carry on the work of those who in the not-so-distant past had the striking courage to overcome fear, ignorance and 'puppet rulers' to create that great but incomplete property of the people—Hydro-Québec."[4]

These are hot words from the restless and charismatic Lévesque, and they are typical of the separatist-left emerging in Québec in the late 1960s.

English Canada, too, has produced economic nationalists, but their words and aspirations seem cool by comparison. When the University League for Social Reform published its important critique, *The Prospect of Change*, in the mid-1960s, this restraint did not go unnoticed. The prospects were there, "in ably argued essays" according to the late Frank Underhill. But this historian, who had been a political activist in the 1930s, was disappointed because "these authors are not challenging us to a new way of life," and because there was "too little fire in sixteen bellies."[5]

The Committee for an Independent Canada embraces all

three national political parties in its membership without having captured the heart or allegiance of any. And it has never really caught the public imagination.

"Buy Back Canada" is a shout of rage, not a call to the race.

The name of Québec's contemporary political party, the Parti Québécois, identifies a separate political process from the rest of Canada; there is no Ontario Party or British Columbia Party. And the emotion-filled name of the Parti Québécois' Economic Manifesto—*Prochaine étape . . . quand nous serons vraiment chez nous* ("Next step . . . when we are truly in our own home")—guarantees a new step in history.

Québec will enter independence with her culture, her history and her national definitions intact.

We in English Canada have been so preoccupied with what Québec's emergence will mean to the rest of Canada, and so convinced that what is happening is somehow unique, that we have not understood it in terms of a common hemispheric history.

There is a powerful thesis, widely known in the United States and throughout Latin America but forgotten in Canada, that the nations of the Western Hemisphere have a strong, common history. The thesis was first outlined in 1932 by the late American historian Herbert Eugene Bolton, a specialist in the history of the Spanish frontiers of the present American Southwest and Mexico.

> In the half-century between 1776 and 1826, practically all of South America and two-thirds of North America became politically independent of Europe and a score of nations came into being. . . .
>
>   . . .Since separation from Europe these nations have been striving on the one hand for national solidarity, political stability and economic well-being, and on the other hand for a satisfactory

adjustment of relations with each other and with the
rest of the world.
   . . .It is my purpose to suggest our national
histories are but phases common to most portions of
the entire Western Hemisphere. . .that much of what
has been written of each national history is but a
thread of a larger strand.[6]

The commonality of our histories began with the
purposes and experiences of European colonial powers in
settling and exploiting the New World. These depended to a
large degree on the region of the Western Hemisphere
where they established colonies, and the ways in which they
responded to the hemisphere's different environments.

The French and English settled mainly in the cool forest
and lake regions of the Northern Hemisphere, and in many
of the tropical Caribbean islands. The Portuguese, armed in
1494 with a fiat from Pope Alexander VI (who thought he
was dividing up Asia), settled in what would become the
subcontinent of Brazil. The Spanish penetrated the islands,
jungles and mountain ranges of the Caribbean, Central and
South America; and the arid backlands of the present
American southwest, which was for more than two
centuries an outreach of the Viceroyalty of New Spain and
the successor Mexican Republic.

All the colonial systems of the New World attempted to
implant similar feudal structures on their various wilderness
domains and over their indigenous peoples. Spain had her
encomienda and the later paramilitary *presidio*. Portugal
had her *capitania*, the English had the quasi-democratic
proprietary grant, and the French had the *seigneury*. These
were all institutions of the mutually shared mercantilist
system, which existed for the benefit of the mother
countries in terms of export of the New World's many
bounties—gold and silver, furs, sugar, timber, cocoa,
molasses and rubber.

We forget how truly great were the achievements of our

European ancestors in overcoming the staggering physical obstacles to colonization. Within a century of the initial Spanish explorations—that is by 1700—Spain had built and settled about 200 cities and towns throughout the New World. To this day, the modern Spanish-American republics of Mexico and Peru dispute which national capital, Lima or Mexico City, was the seat of the first university in the Western Hemisphere. And the two years in question both predate 1600.

The French fur traders and explorers penetrated more than 2,000 miles beyond the tiny colony of New France. They left a permanent mark in the names of the American Midwest—Laramie, Pierre's Hole, Coeur d'Alene, the Nez Percés Indians—and their memory still lives in the claims of occupation scribbled on rocks and in the verbal records of the Indian nations who intermingled with them.

New France emerged as more uniquely American than did the colonies of Spain, Portugal or England. King Louis XIV was primarily concerned with French hegemony in Europe, and so New France lacked the military support from the mother country enjoyed by the other New World settlements. At times during the seventeenth and eighteenth centuries France almost abandoned her tiny empire on the St. Lawrence, leaving the colonists to their own devices.

As a result, the French in the New World became less French and more *canadien*, so much so that it is historically accurate to say that it was *les canadiens* and not French colonials who surrendered to English armies on the Plains of Abraham.

The oldest Québec families identify their origins not from the year their ancestors left France, but from the time their family records first appeared in the parish rolls of the oldest Québec churches.

Professor Marcel Trudel's excellent map of the parishes

of Québec identifies them as *paroisses canadiennes* rather than *paroisses de la Nouvelle France*.

It is understandable that a style of government and a social order much different from those of the parent country emerged.

Professor W.J. Eccles refers to "the aristocratic welfare state" of New France in which the role of the government was "more akin to that of many governments of today" in taking responsibility for the orphans, the poor and the illegitimate children. [7]

In 1669 Intendant Champigny commented on citizen participation in the life of the colony, at a time when there was very little citizen participation in France: "They help each other in a way quite different to the way they do it in France." [8]

Nevertheless, the similarities in the colonial systems, Bolton maintained, were more striking than the differences. Common experiences included competitive struggles for spheres of influence in the New World's land and sea territories, slavery and the appearance of new racial mixtures through intermarriage, the resistance of the Indian throughout the hemisphere to all European intrusions, and the emergence of new economic systems through contact with the frontiers.

Bolton chided Canadian and American historians for seeing the struggle for the continent only in North American terms, as though it had all happened north of the Gulf of Mexico. Exploration and expansion from original coastal settlements into hinterland frontiers took place in South as well as North America. For example, the Brazilian colonial drive from the Atlantic to the Andes was similar to the westward movements in both the United States and Canada.

The expulsion of the Acadians in 1755 was not unique to Canadian history; nor was the immediate reason for it—that

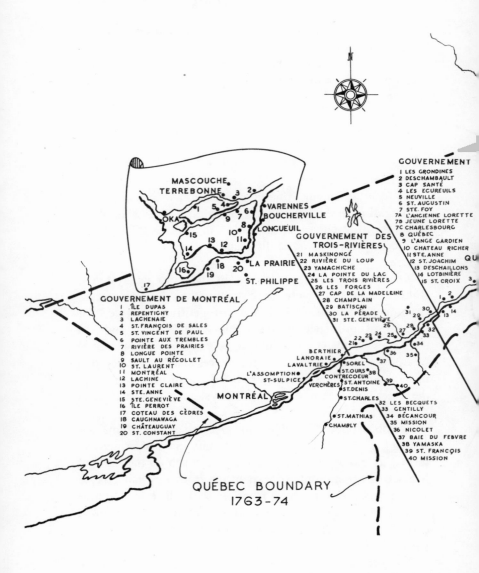

GOUVERNEMENT

1 LES GRONDINES
2 DESCHAMBAULT
3 CAP SANTÉ
4 LES ECUREUILS
5 NEUVILLE
6 ST. AUGUSTIN
7 STE. FOY
7A L'ANCIENNE LORETTE
7B JEUNE LORETTE
7C CHARLESBOURG
8 QUÉBEC
9 L'ANGE GARDIEN
10 CHATEAU RICHER
11 STE. ANNE
12 ST. JOACHIM
13 DESCHAILLONS
14 LOTBINIÈRE
15 ST. CROIX

GOUVERNEMENT DES
TROIS-RIVIÈRES

21 MASKINONGÉ
22 RIVIÈRE DU LOUP
23 YAMACHICHE
24 LA POINTE DU LAC
25 LES TROIS RIVIÈRES
26 LES FORGES
27 CAP DE LA MADELEINE
28 CHAMPLAIN
29 BATISCAN
30 LA PÉRADE
31 STE. GENEVIÈVE

GOUVERNEMENT DE MONTRÉAL

1 ÎLE DUPAS
2 REPENTIGNY
3 LACHENAIE
4 ST. FRANÇOIS DE SALES
5 ST. VINCENT DE PAUL
6 POINTE AUX TREMBLES
7 RIVIÈRE DES PRAIRIES
8 LONGUE POINTE
9 SAULT AU RÉCOLLET
10 ST. LAURENT
11 MONTRÉAL
12 LACHINE
13 POINTE CLAIRE
14 STE. ANNE
15 STE. GENEVIÈVE
16 ÎLE PERROT
17 COTEAU DES CÈDRES
18 CAUGHNAWAGA
19 CHÂTEAUGUAY
20 ST. CONSTANT

32 LES BECQUETS
33 GENTILLY
34 BÉCANCOUR
35 MISSION
36 NICOLET
37 BAIE DU FEBVRE
38 YAMASKA
39 ST. FRANÇOIS
40 MISSION

QUÉBEC BOUNDARY
1763-74

PAROISSES CANADIENNES / CANADIAN PARISHES 1763
The parish lists of the churches of Québec record a French population explosion
from 70,000 in 1760 to about four million in 1950, due chiefly to the high
birthrate rather than immigration from France.

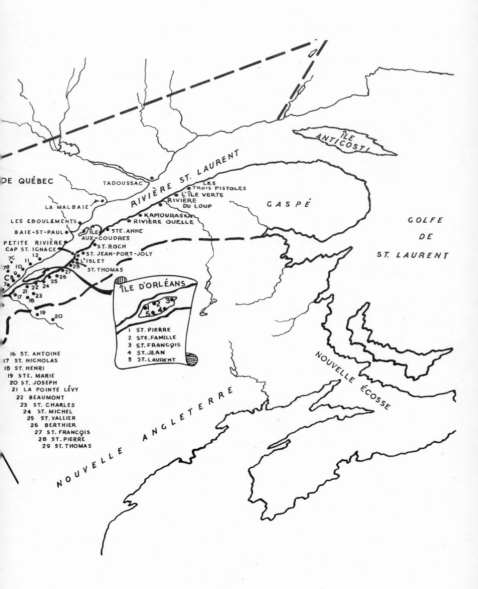

Courtesy of Marcel Trudel; developed in *Atlas Historique,* Les Presses de l'Université Laval, Québec, 1968. Adapted by Reg. Hewson.

is, a territorial conflict between two European colonial empires. In 1635 the Portuguese, advancing inland from the South Atlantic, routed a growing Spanish Jesuit mission colony in what is now Paraguay, forcing 12,000 Spanish and Indian inhabitants to flee.

A vital part of colonial expansion in the Western Hemisphere was the use of slavery as a source of cheap labor. All four of the European colonial systems supported the importation of African blacks to the New World possessions, although it was most common in the tropical colonies and viceroyalties of South and Central America and the Caribbean, and in the southern United States.

Latin American historian Philip C. Brooks elaborated another facet of the Bolton thesis: "Nowhere else in the world, with the exception of South Africa and Australia, have European peoples so completely replaced or absorbed native civilizations. Nowhere else has European culture been so completely transplanted. . . . In China and India . . . Europeans have settled, but the life is still Chinese and Indian."[9]

The resistance of the Indian—Aztec, Inca, Navajo, Ojibwa, Algonquin—to all the penetrating European civilizations has persisted into the twentieth century. We are witnessing it in the determined resistance of Canada's northern Indian and Inuit societies to the newest and most pervasive of the white man's many technologies: the oil and gas pipeline.

Shortly before the invasion of pipelines in the Western Hemisphere, an Ecuadorian historian wrote: "The psychological resistance of the Indian. . .was and remains to this day, in his repugnance to the assimilation of the white man's civilization, one of the most extraordinary phenomena in human history. This resistance has lasted for ages and has the frightening implications of collective suicide."[10]

Though Professor Bolton did not say so in precise terms,

the racial interbreeding in the Americas is another example of the commonality of our American historical experience.

The psychological resistance of the Indian to the white man notwithstanding, the association of Indian, white settler and black slave in the New World inevitably produced many new and in some instances dynamic communities of racially mixed North and South Americans.

The Canadian experience with the Métis—the intermarriage or cohabitation of Indian with French and Scottish settlers—was a far from unique experience in racial union.

The mestizo (Indian and white) and mulatto (black and white) racial mixtures of Central and South America are widespread.

Brazil prides itself on being a genuine multiracial society. This is true of that huge nation's lower classes, although less true of the industrial and military elites. Nevertheless Brazilians inherited the Portuguese tendency towards miscegenation and racial intermarriage, and in colonial Brazil African slaves were often integrated through marriage and cohabitation into the families of rich planters. The Indian massacres characteristic of the Spanish colonies in the eighteenth century and the American western plains never took place.[11]

Jamaica, to cite another example, is not an island of blacks, but a hodge-podge of many races—black, white, Chinese and East Indian—who came to the island either voluntarily or as slaves. "White" refers not only to Jamaicans of British descent but to the so-called Syrians—families of Lebanese stock who, like the East Indians, came to Jamaica and the other Caribbean islands to trade.

A final common experience of all colonial empires and the nations which evolved from them was the exploitation of the frontier by foreign investment and immigrant manpower.

Bolton called the frontier "a powerful nationalizing force." Canadians, Americans, Brazilians, Argentines and

Mexicans alike have experienced the drive by dynamic capitalists to build railways, mines, plantations and ranches in the wilderness. There have been opportunities for social experimentation, too, resulting in the American melting pot, the modernization of the Mexican Indian, and the "New Canadians" of many ethnic origins.

By 1900, all the larger New World colonial regions had become politically independent nations. But the industrial revolution had forced them into a new, postcolonial dependency on the European powers, whose factories and growing populations demanded the raw materials and food resources of the New World.

Canadians will understand the development of Argentina during this phase, because it was similar to our own. Professor Marc-A. Blain, a historian at l'Université de Montréal, explains: "These two nations, Canada and Argentina, became the archetypes of the new countries . . .so vast that one imagines them to be limitless. . .little by little they defined their role as frontier regions of the old continent."[12]

The Anglo-Argentine meat trade between 1880 and 1930, with its creation of a food-preservation technology in the form of the meat-packing plant and the refrigerated cargo ship, had a pronounced and lasting influence on the emergence of the modern Argentine society and economy. The parallel in Canada was the wheat boom of the early 1900s, which developed hand-in-hand with the settlement of the prairies.

The reliance of both countries on changing world markets not only directed their early economic growth as new states, but encouraged the development of elite business classes and created the need for massive immigration.

The "strong back and weak mind" invective which Canadian immigration minister Sir Clifford Sifton applied to the Slavic immigrants arriving in the Canadian West in the early 1900s had its parallel in the woeful exploitation of the rural gaucho and the urban Italian immigrant factory worker in Argentina.[13]

The common Argentine-Canadian experience in nation-building is best seen in the extension of both nations to their polar limits—Argentina in Antarctica, Canada in the Arctic.

One must admit that the Argentines, with fewer resources and less modern marine technology than Canada, have made a more determined polar thrust. Undeterred by the overlapping claims of large European powers—Britain, the USSR, France and Norway—as well as by those of her Chilean neighbor and the U.S.A., Argentina has carved out her wedge of Antarctic ice and snow. She justifies sovereignty under the effective occupation principle, having established over the years more than a dozen tiny military and scientific stations in the claimed sector. Argentina also contests ownership of the British crown colony of the Falkland Islands, which are presently inhabited mostly by fiercely anti-Argentine Scottish sheepherders.

In spite of the large boost to Argentine nationalism from two exposures to Peronism (for which we mercifully have no parallel Canadian experience), Argentines have made interminable efforts to catch the brass ring of national identity, an exercise we Canadians know all about. These words, reminiscent of a Bruce Hutchinson or an Abraham Rotstein, were spoken by Argentine political scientist José Luís Romero in 1946: "It would be difficult to state what we Argentines are. The Argentine soul is an enigma because the collective personality of the nation is still in the process of elaboration."[14] Sound familiar?

If we accept Bolton's theory that the New World colonies have evolved in remarkably similar ways, the eventual separation of Québec becomes quite logical. With the sole exception of Puerto Rico, all of the former Spanish and Portuguese colonies have achieved independence. Does it not seem natural that Québec, with a territory and a resource base far surpassing those of many Latin republics, plus a language and culture that have been fiercely preserved through two centuries of English domination, should also desire sovereignty?

Canada in the postwar era has remained largely oblivious to her hemispheric role. We think in "Pan-American" terms only when we are forced to by events like the Cuban missile crisis of 1962, or when it is clearly to our advantage to establish Third-World trading partners in Latin America. Vincent Massey's elitist book *On Being Canadian*, published shortly after World War II, discussed the theme of Canada and Pan-Americanism. That Canadian of another age, with his patrician views of Canadian society, saw very little value for Canada in Pan-American relationships. "In this area, we can find little or no unity, cultural, economic or strategic," he wrote. "The 'Western Hemisphere' complex which regards North and South America as a unit can seriously mislead us."[15]

The start of the cold war, and Canada's resulting new role in the North Atlantic Treaty Organization in 1949, justified Mr. Massey's claim for our orientation towards Europe, the British Commonwealth and historic Old World connections.

John W. Holmes, a Canadian scholar of international affairs, looked at this direction two decades later and concluded: "Two wars, NATO and the United States sent Canada looking for allies its own size, although Canadians still suffer from a myopic concentration on North Atlantic affairs."[16]

At the same time, Holmes rejects even more strongly than Massey any attachment to the Pan-American concept. "Dumbellists on both sides of the Atlantic, if queried about the Canadian role, had a habit of suggesting that Canadians should run off and find happiness in their regional bundle. Sometimes this meant simple 'union' with a nation ten times Canada's size; sometimes. . .it wrapped Canadians up with their neighbors in Paraguay in accordance with prevalent myths about the 'naturalness' of hemispheric ties.''[17]

Neither Massey in the 1940s nor Holmes in the 1960s investigated the Canadian corollary to the Bolton thesis; that the heirs of the French, the fourth major European civilizing force in the New World, are prepared to set themselves up as an American nation.

For too long—indeed, throughout the history of our foreign policy—Canada has denied its place among the nations of the Western Hemisphere.

Membership in the old Pan American Union, the predecessor to the Organization of American States formed in 1889, or even in the OAS itself, was not for us. The "Inter-American system," that phrase beloved of many generations of U.S. congressmen and continentalist Latin American intellectuals, was too much for Canadians.

We preferred to remain more European than American, and to emphasize our ties with two global commonwealths, neither of which are indigenous to this hemisphere: the British Commonwealth and the more recently structured *francophonie* (French-speaking) community.

Better that Canada work within the British Empire we knew, and which had eased us into full nationhood, than join forces with the American empire whose republicanism we still mistrusted, or with the more distant Latin American republics.

Canadian nineteenth- and twentieth-century suspicion of Pan-Americanism has deep historical roots.

Generations of Canadian schoolchildren, some of whom would become diplomats, politicians, business leaders and opinion makers, were raised on British-oriented history books that demeaned Spain and the role of Spanish civilization in history. Their dubious clichés—for example, that the defeat of the Spanish Armada in 1588 precipitated the decline of the Spanish empire and the rise of the British—were not likely to encourage fair or objective appreciation of the Hispanic societies of Latin America.

One of Canada's greatest international diplomats, the late Lester B. Pearson, in spite of his support for ultimate Canadian entry into the Organization of American States, always dealt with Latin Americans in a broader and more impersonal context than purely hemispheric affairs. He knew leading diplomats from Latin America and the Caribbean through the United Nations and the World Bank, but these associations were always at arm's length and never involved the personal intimacy which Latin Americans prefer when dealing with politicians, diplomats and businessmen from the north. Pearson was the product of a Protestant manse in anti-Catholic southern Ontario, and was raised within the Calvinist tradition that had perpetuated the belief, century after century, that Spaniards were cruel and corrupt in Central and South America because they were Catholic.

Canadian foreign policy towards the hemisphere has often appeared to be an extension, unconscious or otherwise, of the pietistic and self-assured Calvinism that influenced Canada so deeply during its formative years.

In our typically quiet and arrogant way, Canadians have supported *la leyenda negra* ("the black legend"), as Spanish and Spanish-American scholars call the Anglo-Saxon, anti-Catholic crusade against Spanish civilization.

As recently as 1972, an especially competent ambassador from a Spanish-speaking Caribbean republic despaired openly to the author about the bias against Latins that he sensed in his dealings with the Canadian Department of External Affairs.

The bias against Spanish America was easily transferred to Québec. English-Canadians have been taught that French society and culture in Catholic Québec were more backward and corrupt than in Ontario or western Canada. The defeat of the French on the Plains of Abraham in 1759 took on the same meaning as the defeat of Spain at sea in 1588; the decline of Catholic empires was as inevitable as the rise of the Protestant and British empires.

Out of such atrocious historical biases grew the present deep-set prejudices and lingering sense of Anglo-Saxon superiority which are at the base of the separatist resistance to all English-Canadian institutions in Québec.

Canadians have in the past been peculiarly blind to events in the countries of Latin America. In the same way that we have not understood the emergence of Québec since 1960 in the Quiet Revolution, many modern experiments of a similar kind in the hemisphere have also escaped us.

During the last half-century these have included a genuine social revolution in Mexico; the building of social democracies in Chile, Uruguay, Venezuela and Costa Rica (even though the first two were destroyed by military coups in 1970 and 1973); and, in Brazil, a determined thrust to become a major world power on the basis of growing economic strength.

To borrow any kind of model in the nation-building process from a continent plagued by military coups, poverty and revolution, would seem to us incongruous. To believe that another democracy in our hemisphere in any way resembled our own would be, to say the least, intellectual licence. Not until social democracy was destroyed in some of these nations, as happened in Chile in September 1973, did their roles as emerging societies come to view in Canada.

For years Canadians working or studying in remote, mountain-bound Chile, a country as far away from Canada as the People's Republic of China, told us that Chile had built a social democracy. An identifiable Chilean middle class of professionals, entrepreneurs, managers and government officials had maintained one of the few free societies in Latin America.

Isolated from us by the Spanish language so few Canadians can speak, Chile pursued a tortuous course into Marxism in 1970, then suffered a calamitous military coup. Chile's ordeal after September 11, 1973 would affect us in spite of ourselves. The Chileans who had served or sympathized with a Marxist government faced persecution and worse. Though they were good citizen potential, educated bourgeoisie and not illiterate coolies or jungle tribesmen, their plight and their need for sanctuary confused and angered Canadian officials and public.

Domestic pressure groups, mainly members of the political left, demanded immediate entry for as many Chileans as possible without too much concern about their left-wing political affiliations. Other groups cautioned gloomily against the influx of potential subversives.

The Canadian government took some time to make up its mind what to do. Screening teams were finally sent to the Canadian embassy in Santiago, with only the most cursory knowledge of the labyrinthian ideologies of the Chilean political left, to pick out the desirable potential immigrants as they saw fit. Thousands of Chileans were ultimately given entry into Canada.

The Chilean experience not only focused Canada's attention on South America; it taught Canadians that a refugee crisis originating in this hemisphere could be just as heartrending for the victims, and just as demanding of our hospitality, as the previous ones in Europe and Africa that brought Hungarian, Czech and Ugandan East Indian refugees to our shores.

Venezuela has taught Canada a different kind of lesson: that measures to promote economic nationalism are not unique to Canada but have already been introduced in many leading Latin American republics.

During the fall of 1973, Hugo Pérez la Salvia, then Venezuelan minister of hydrocarbons and minerals, made it clear to the Canadian government that Venezuela would prefer, in future, to negotiate international agreements on oil supply through an agency of the Canadian government similar to the Venezuelan state oil corporation.

At that time Venezuela was preparing for the final nationalization of her oil industry (which took place on January 1, 1976), and wished to replace the large private oil companies as the major negotiators on oil exports. These were the former Creole Petroleum Company in Venezuela and Imperial Oil Limited in Canada, both Exxon Corporation subsidiaries, and the former Shell de Venezuela and Shell Canada Limited.

Before total nationalization, the Venezuelan government took part in an oil industry which like its Canadian counterpart was more than 70 percent foreign-owned, through a small but powerful state agency called CVP— Corporación Venezolana de Petróleo (Venezuelan Petroleum Corporation).

Canada did not have a state oil corporation to fulfill the requirement of the Venezuelans, although a National Petroleum Corporation Act had been in the process of development.

Petro-Canada, formed in 1975 as a crown corporation, appears to have been modeled on the Venezuelan corporation, although the CVP had much wider powers, including participation at the retail level. Petro-Canada has authority to engage in activities similar to those initiated by CVP, such as operating a state tanker fleet—in Canada's case to ship offshore Arctic oil if it is ever discovered in quantity. It is also deeply involved in frontier exploration and drilling, in trying to expand our refining capacity, and in fighting off attacks from the Calgary community of private oil industry which resents Petro-Canada's presence and competition.

The association of Petro-Canada with PetroVen, the new Venezuelan state oil corporation formed on January 1, 1976, continues through such activities as conferences for senior oil technicians. The first of these, held by the

Petroleum Society of the Canadian Institute of Mining and Metallurgy in Edmonton, in May 1977, investigated common problems in extracting oil from the Alberta and Orinoco River tar sands.

Thus, little by little, Canada is being forced into an awareness of her dynamic Latin neighbours to the south.

Before the federal election of October 1972, Prime Minister Trudeau, in a soon-forgotten speech in Toronto, said that Canadians must have "a will to hold together." That will is being challenged by Québec, a part of Canada whose geographic and hemispheric identity was always certain.

English-Canadian definitions of Canada, whether as a middle power, North Atlantic nation, monarchy or dominion, have always drawn us into the orbit of our Atlantic, European and British interests.

Yet part of our country has a deep sense of sanctity about the hemispheric home, an intangible but nevertheless powerful association which English-Canadians have never been able to understand or accept.

One suspects that when Québec separates, English-Canadians who once asked, with a mixture of arrogance, dismay and bewilderment, "What does Québec want?" will ask for generations after the split, "Why did Québec go?"

NOTES

1. In spite of its Caribbean locale, Spanish-speaking Puerto Rico shares some startling similarities with Québec. During the boomy 1950s and '60s both markets were penetrated by the subsidiaries of hundreds of U.S. parent companies. The English-speaking management of the multinationals resisted learning Spanish in Puerto Rico as much as they did French in Québec, while Puerto Rican and Québec workers chafed under a system which compelled them to learn English to get jobs.

    Puerto Rico's small Independentista party still wins less

than five percent of the vote in elections, but is encouraged by Castro's Cuba to break the lucrative but culturally stultifying American connection. Puerto Rican students, artists and intellectuals express separatist sentiments similar to those expressed in Québec. At the same time a Puerto Rican middle class which has benefited from association with the United States and from American citizenship denounces the independentistas, just as the urban middle class of Québec, which benefits from the federal connection as a province of Canada, resists separatism. John D. Harbron, "Le Québec et le réveil des sociétés latines," Cité libre, March 1965, pp. 21-24.

2. Jean Bruchési, A History of Canada, trans. R. W. W. Robertson (Toronto: Clarke, Irwin, 1950), p. 279.

3. Hubert Aquin, Prochain épisode (Montreal: Le Cercle du livre de France, 1965), p. 74.

4. Paul Sauriol, The Nationalization of Electric Power (Montreal: Harvest House, 1962), p. 10.

5. Frank H. Underhill, review of Prospect of Change, Globe and Mail, March 13, 1965.

6. Lewis Hanke, ed., Do the Americas Have a Common History? A Critique of the Bolton Thesis (New York: Alfred A. Knopf, 1966), p.79.

7. W. J. Eccles, Canadian Society During the French Regime (Montreal: Harvest House, 1968), p. 30.

8. Ibid, p. 30.

9. Philip C. Brooks, "Do the Americas Share a Common History?" Revista de Historia de América, no. 33 (1952).

10. Frank Tannenbaum, Ten Keys to Latin America (New York: Alfred A. Knopf, 1962), p. 39.

11. The recent brutal treatment of Brazil's diminishing aboriginal Amazonian tribes by the Amazon developers, and the genocide allegedly practiced by the military, are definitely not within the historic pattern of racial harmony which has been more marked in Brazil than in any other South American republic. Thousands of Brazilians have been shocked by such atrocities and even the semi-controlled Brazilian press has reacted strongly, forcing the military governments of Brazil to investigate their own activities in the Amazon.

12. Marc-A. Blain, "Le rôle de la dépendance externe et des structures sociales dans l'économie frumentaire du Canada et

de l'Argentine (1880-1930), *Revue d'histoire de l'Amérique française* 26 (September 1972), p. 239.

13. After 1930 Argentina used grain elevators designed and built by C. D. Howe, who was a leading grain elevator designer before joining the Liberal government in 1935, and subsequently one of the most powerful industrialists and politicians in Canadian history. Howe returned to Argentina in 1953 as head of Canada's first ministerial trade mission to Latin America since 1941. John D. Harbron, "Ottawa Reappraises State Corporations," *Business Week*, November 19, 1960, pp. 185-92.

14. John D. Harbron, "Argentina's National Search," *Toronto Telegram*, May 13, 1970.

15. Vincent Massey, *On Being Canadian* (Toronto: J. M. Dent and Sons, 1946), p. 193.

16. John W. Holmes, *The Better Part of Valour: Essays on Canadian Diplomacy* (Toronto: McClelland and Stewart, Carleton Library, no. 49, 1967), p. 30.

17. Ibid., p. 124.

2

The Political Language of the Québec Nation State

2

At last there may come an hour in our life. . .a day of
wholesome retaliation when it will be possible for us
to say to ourselves as others do, I have a land of my
own. I have a soil of my own. I have a future of my
own.

> Abbé Lionel Groulx,
> *Why We Are Divided*

English-Canadians will continue to ignore and misun-
derstand the dynamic nature of French-Canadian
nationalism because most of them have not read the
literature of separatism and never will.

That literature remains as important to the mainstream of
contemporary Canadian political thought as the essays of
the late Frank Underhill on Canadian liberalism, the
speeches of J. S. Woodsworth on a Canadian social
democracy or the statements and essays of Pierre Elliott
Trudeau on Canadian federalism.

The literature of separatism tells English-Canadians they
are in a conflict against a national ideology with few verbal
weapons for the combat. Ideology is at the heart of
French-Canadian nationalist thought and literature; English

Canada rejects ideology in its political thought and political process.

Québec's separatist writing has had a common theme— the creation of a new independent nation on the banks of the St. Lawrence River.

The challenge of creating a separate Québec homeland is a *cri de coeur* English-Canadians have never understood.

The Québec separatists of the 1920s and '30s were Catholic, visionary and reactionary. They rallied to the call of history, race, the faith and the cradle.

"Two words express the profound substance of our being," wrote Abbé Lionel Groulx, "Catholic and French. . .we are of a divine race, we are sons of God."[1]

The modern separatist is socialist and interventionist. He rejects church and family values for the sterner secular values of modern political doctrine.

"Our escape into the past, into legend has been only a neurotic mechanism of self-defense against the encroachments. . .of the Holy Church," writes a militant separatist in the early 1970s.[2]

Notre maître le passé ("Our master the past"), the words of inspiration for the reactionary nationalist, are rejected by the modern separatist.

Québec's contemporary ideology of independence is similar to the determination of a Third World society to emerge on its own terms, whether or not that emergence contains the seeds of self-destruction, self-sacrifice and loss of economic momentum.

The extreme-left separatists use harsh neo-Marxist language:

> The French Canadian society was always a minority and an inferior society, a colonial society where the role of the colonizer was played at first by England, then by English Canada.
> This was the constant which traversed the different regimes. Collectively we have never known liberty.

> We have always been a dependent colonial people.
> We have never known history except that of
> others. . .that condition of being colonized as
> minorities has made us what we are. . .and is the first
> reason for our alienation.[3]

The fathers of Québec's literature of separatism are
Jules-Paul Tardivel, whose curious and arcane novel bears
the flat title *Pour la patrie* ("For the Fatherland"), and
economic nationalist Errol Bouchette, who coined the
famous motto *Maîtres chez nous* ("Masters in our own
house") about seventy years ago.

Tardivel's novel, published in 1895, centers on a
Catholic fanatic and separatist politician who enters into a
spiritual agreement with St. Joseph to help him form a
French and Catholic "Republic of New France" by the year
1946. It is full of the worst kind of bigotry, misplaced
heroics and fanaticism. Tardivel sees Masons, Jews and
English-Canadian businessmen in Montreal as the committed enemies of a theocratic state on the St. Lawrence.

Yet his extreme faith, and his assurance that prayer and
subservience to a heavenly order will bring him his earthly
goal, were not unseemly in the Québec of 1895.

Catholicism as a religious and political force was on the
defensive in Canada at that time. The Manitoba Schools
Question was a burning issue, just how intense we can guess
from the battle over the use of French by air traffic
controllers during 1976 and 1977. The growing commercial
power of the Westmount Protestant business barons was
beginning to concern Québec writers. In fact, Tardivel saw
then what later separatists would also realize—that the
English-Canadians in the Québec economy would do more
to forestall a separate state than would the distant British
Empire of which Canada in 1895 was an important part.

Tardivel's religious extremism and high romanticism did
not prevent him from defining the future Québec state in

words not unlike those of neo-Marxist authors (if you omit the strong reliance on Divine Providence): "Our people have aspired towards that goal, an independent New France, as long as we have existed and Divine Providence has led us towards it across a thousand obstacles. . . .The predestined hour is sounding at last. It is time for us to take our place among the nations of the earth."[4]

The essays of Errol Bouchette, who wrote at the turn of the century, were the intellectual precursor of the Economic Manifesto of the Parti Québécois seven decades later.

Bouchette was the French-Canadian Walter Gordon of his time. His writing expressed his frustration about the growing foreign control over local industries and resources and advocated that Québec work towards economic sovereignty.

Bouchette's essays were published in a new edition in early 1977 with an introduction by Rodrigue Tremblay, himself an economic nationalist and industrial development minister in the cabinet of the Parti Québécois.

The reactionary and strongly Catholic nationalist movement in the Québec of the 1920s and '30s was led by Abbé Lionel Groulx, professor and historian, who Claude Ryan once called the spiritual father of modern Québec. Groulx proposed a French *République de la Laurentie* on the banks of the St. Lawrence, a New World republic linked to the church and ancient values of land and race.

He also fathered the concept of *souveraineté association* currently proposed by René Lévesque. Though he wrote long before the era of common markets, Groulx envisioned his République as a new state within the Canadian Confederation similar to the Republic of Ireland, created in 1921 as a new state with direct economic ties to the British Empire. He came close to economic thinking when he wrote in 1943: "We are the arch which links east and west. By the river we guard the great door to the sea; through our territory we give passage to the transcontinental railways on their way to the ports of the Atlantic and the Pacific. . .there may be richer lands than ours; nevertheless we possess some of the most opulent riches of Canada and of America."[5]

Québec nationalism has been strongly influenced by European ideologies, from the fascism of the 1930s to the neo-Marxism of the 1970s.

The Action française movement which flourished in the early 1920s attacked the domination of Québec's cultural and commercial life by foreign interests and the erosion of the French language and culture. But it was also colored by the dark elements of the European right-wing political movements: anti-Semitism and a fascination with the corporate states of Portugal, Austria and Italy, and of Spain after Generalíssimo Franco's military victory in 1939.

The movement's right-wing journal, *l'Action française*, borrowed its name and, one suspects, many of its rightist ideas from the *Action française* movement of Charles Maurras, a French fascist whose political ideas were promoted by Vichy France in the early 1940s.

A major study of Québec's politics by two authors who admire neo-Marxist solutions comments:

> The traditional right-wing nationalism of *l'Action française* and *l'Action nationale* [which succeeded *l'Action française*] always held out the possibility and the hope for an independent nation and never rested content with the subordinate positions of French Canadians within Québec and Canada.
>
> It made the intellectuals of Québec aware of the fragility of their culture and the changing values of the masses.[6]

In the progression of Québec's nationalist thought, her writers have examined Latin American republics as allies in the sense of their common "Latin" heritage.

In the 1920s and '30s, the reactionary thinkers of Québec

RÉPUBLIQUE DE LA NOUVELLE FRANCE 1946.

SUGGESTED PARTIAL CONTROL OVER "NEW QUÉBEC" LATER UNGAVA REGION.

In 1895 Jules-Paul Tardivel envisioned a République de la Nouvelle France which would be formed by the year 1946. The republic would be expansionist, with control over the District of Ungava (author's concept).

RÉPUBLIQUE DE LA LAURENTIE   CIRCA 1920.

RELATED FRENCH - LANGUAGE COMMUNITIES IN N. ONTARIO, MANITOBA, SASKATCHEWAN.

In the 1920s Lionel Groulx and other nationalists envisioned a République de la Laurentie, which would have strong ties with French-language communities in Northern Ontario, Manitoba and Saskatchewan (author's concept).

visualized Latin America as a large counterweight to the growing continental power of the United States. The prosperity and unprecedented boom of the 1920s started the flow of American investment into Canada which continues to the present time and which has deeply concerned Québec's economic nationalists.

The same penetrations were taking place in Latin America as the United States sought the raw materials of the hemisphere for its expanding industries. Anti-American sentiment was aroused in Hispanic America identical to that emerging in Québec. The materialist values of the United States were seen as corrupting the deep-set spiritual values of all Catholic societies in the Western Hemisphere.

Emile Bruchési, brother of the well-known conservative French-Canadian historian Jean Bruchési, in "The French State and Latin America," described a French nation in Québec which would be forced to look for allies in Latin America "against the covetous greed of the 'Giant of the North.' " In this Latin hemisphere, he claimed, were several opponents of the Anglo-Saxon civilization of the United States; "cousins by race, by mentality, but cousins who do not know us."[7]

Admiration in Québec for the Catholic and conservative tradition in the Spanish Americas reached its peak after Franco's victory in the Spanish Civil War in April 1939.

Franco's Catholic and Christian Spain had won against the communist anti-Christ of the defeated Republican government, and in its first decade the Franco regime carried this message of Catholic reaction from the motherland to the former Spanish New World colonies.

The Consejo de Hispanidad (Council for Hispanicity), an agency of Franco's government, was established in Madrid in the early 1940s. It encouraged the role of Spanish priests in Latin America as teachers and administrators of the private schools for the children and descendants of original Spanish immigrants. It also distributed books and films and sent lecturers to propagate the role of Spain in the Americas.

This influence predominated in those republics—particularly Cuba, Peru, Colombia, Argentina and Chile—where vigorous and rich communities of Spanish immigrants had openly supported Franco with funds and volunteers during the Spanish Civil War.

In 1940 Franco's promoters of Spanish racial superiority established the Día de la Raza (Day of the Race) on the anniversary of Christopher Columbus's first landing in America. This event is still celebrated each October 12th in many Latin areas of the Western Hemisphere.

In Québec, in the 1930s, the secretive and racist Société Saint-Jean-Baptiste was growing in power, with devotion to the Catholic faith and proof of French origin as prerequisites for membership.

The thoughts of Franco's propagandists, published in church periodicals and conservative newspapers throughout Latin America, echoed those of Abbé Groulx and the brothers Bruchési in Québec: "For the America of our culture, our faith, our blood we wish more than just living together. . .we desire unity. . .of mind. . .of economy . . .of power. . . .We desire to put an end to 'Monroeism' in order to put in its place our affirmation, 'the Spanish world for the Spanish.' "[8]

Nostalgia for an imperial past, and a New World heritage of faith and racial purity, were thus shared by Spanish America and Québec.

But in 1937 André Laurendeau, who would strongly influence the ideas of Pierre Trudeau and his fellow social reformers of the early 1950s, returned from France to become the new editor of *l'Action nationale*, which succeeded *l'Action française*. He had developed new ideas for change in Québec from his association with the great contemporary French writers—Maritain, Malraux and Camus—and he ended *l'Action nationale's* support of racism and European fascist systems which his father Arthur

Laurendeau had encouraged as previous editor. (André Laurendeau later proposed that Canada appoint a commission to study bilingualism and biculturalism, and was made one of the chairmen of that commission.)

The fascism and romanticism of the Québec of the 1930s and '40s were gradually eroded by the events of World War II, the growing industrialization of the 1950s and the Quiet Revolution of the 1960s.

The churchmen and right-wing intellectuals of the 1920s and '30s had wished to recapture the rural past. The postwar generations, especially those with intense separatist ideas, wished to see provincial institutions created in new molds. And as new ideas for social reform gained momentum in Québec, the influence of the church diminished. The Québec church continued to link hands with repressive political leadership, unable to countenance the experiments in social democracy or the Christian-Marxist dialogue which were becoming vital aspects of Latin American Catholicism. No party for social reform would develop from the Québec church as the Christian Democratic movement did in Chile, Venezuela and Argentina. The literature of social change of the 1950s grew outside the doors of the church.

In 1950 a group of liberal reformers, aroused by the stifling political and religious atmosphere of the Duplessis era, founded *Cité libre*, a magazine of intellectual protest which would have a clear effect on the course of the Quiet Revolution.

Most of the original *citélibristes*, including co-founders Pierre Elliott Trudeau, Gérard Pelletier, Pierre Juneau and Maurice Sauvé, had long since abandoned the Québec scene to enter federal politics. None of these men were separatists; they called for a social democratic system in a Québec within Canada. Professor Paul Painchaud has identified them as "a new elite in Québec not like the traditional elite, [but] state-oriented, founded on the concept of modernity, antichurch and seeing the new culture as a 'Québec culture.' ''[9]

The later wave of Québec radicals, who saw the separation of Québec in terms of a Third World liberation movement, accused the *citélibristes* of settling for *rattrapage*, the catching-up of the old order rather than its complete replacement.

Professor Ronald Sutherland, in his superb comparison of the roots of the English- and French-Canadian novel, describes the malaise underlying the separatist era which began in the late 1960s and has accelerated ever since:

> It is the genuine desire for group self-determination which is shared by thousands, perhaps millions of French Canadians who nevertheless refuse to declare themselves Separatists. These people are the confused masses. They know there is something wrong. They feel frustrated and dehumanized, manipulated by a system which they vaguely identify with English Canada and the United States.[10]

Perhaps the reason why English-Canadians fail to comprehend the political novels of Hubert Aquin, Claude Jasmin, Jacques Godbout, Pierre Gravel, and the unrestrained extremism of Pierre Vallières, is because their imagery relates to an entirely Québécois experience of frustration and anger which English Canadians will never share.

For example, English Canadians often take for granted that the modern separatist is inspired by the ideals of the French Revolution.

But the French Revolution is not a part of the political heritage of Québec. For the novelists of separatism, *les québécois* are a race apart. They share a separateness as incomprehensible to English Canadians as were the views of revolutionary black leaders in the United States of the mid-1960s. In fact, the analogy of French Canadians as the "white niggers of America," popularized in Pierre Vallières' book of the same name, is a recurrent theme of separatist novels.

This peculiar yet pervasive sense of wretchedness has been borrowed in large amounts from the gloomy and desperate writings of the late Frantz Fanon. His revolutionary classic, *The Wretched of the Earth*, was written in part in Algeria during the war of liberation against France in the late 1950s and early '60s.

The feeling of oppression in separatist literature is more than a literary mechanism. Both Aquin and Vallières have written at one time from prison. Aquin was incarcerated for alleged support of the FLQ during the massive police arrest of French-Canadian leftist intellectuals during the FLQ crisis in the fall of 1970. No contemporary English-Canadian novelist has written from an imprisonment incurred for his political beliefs.

Hubert Aquin was the most pessimistic novelist of separatism. He took his own life in March 1977, leaving behind a stream-of-consciousness style of writing the content of which is almost incomprehensible to the English-Canadian.

Was self-destruction his personal response to a Québec society which he believed had already destroyed itself? "The reward of the warrior undone is depression," he wrote. "The reward of national depression—this is my failure."[11]

But this new separatist generation does not consist only of novelists and polemicists, for it has access to a wide range of media. Where the essays on "functional politics" for *Cité libre* had been written in the living rooms of Montreal's upper-class Outremont, the bars, theatres, college auditoriums and movie houses have become the larger and more boisterous stages for the call of the *indépendantistes*. There are dramatists like Michel Tremblay, television stars like Lise Payette (later consumer affairs minister of

Québec), performers like Gilles Vigneault, Pauline Julien, Robert Charlebois, Yvon Deschamps.

In the forefront of this bubbling Québec cultural world are most of the key members of the new Parti Québécois cabinet. Claude Morin, Jacques-Yvan Morin, Rodrigue Tremblay, Guy Joron and Camille Laurin have all written books during the mid and late 1970s.

Energy Minister Joron's brittle and funny book, *Salaire minimum annuel $1 million! ou la course à la folie* ("Minimum Annual Salary One Million Dollars or The Race to Madness"), was scarcely in print when the author was elevated to the cabinet.[12]

René Lévesque's *Option Québec*, published in 1968, outlines his proposals for *souveraineté association*, a common market between an independent Québec and a postsecessionist Canada.

The many elements of the media—publishing, theatre, film, radio and television—offer a much broader base for the creation of a permanent message of dissent than anything in the past.

Moreover, the ideological influences from abroad today are more persuasive than were those of forty or fifty years ago.

Where the corporate states of Latin Europe appealed only to the well-educated Catholic leaders and writers of forty years ago, the sweeping social revolutions of our time in Algeria, China, Vietnam and Cuba appeal to a much wider and more activist community of radicals.

What was wrought in Algiers, Havana and even in Hanoi (which many Québec performers and writers have seen for themselves)—couldn't it also be brought to pass in Québec City?

Need Castro's Cuba be the only liberated Latin society in the hemisphere, the only *território libre de las Américas* ("free territory of the Americas")?

Nevertheless, Québec's artistic community of novelists,

dramatists and poets of separatism tend to be mesmerized by an ideology of their own making. It is a mélange of deep personal cynicism about the status quo in Québec and unrealistic romanticization of the totalitarian regimes they admire.

While they shout "libération" from the pages of militant journals and Montreal nightclub stages, the literary exponents of a semi-authoritarian separatist state in Québec do not talk about the self-sacrifice or the cost to the individual of building a new society.

The Québécois are not Vietnamese, Algerians, Chinese or even Cubans. They are now a part of the North American world of affluence and consumer expectations. What of the Florida vacation, the suburban home, the color television, new car in the garage, the good life in Québec? How deep will sacrifice go?

The political and economic framework of a Québec republic has already been visualized and spelled out by the economists, politicians and public administrators committed to the new nation. Though they have been inspired by the message of separation, they are also highly pragmatic.

The model for a Republic of Québec which will survive and flourish in the North American context was defined in the early 1970s in the Economic Manifesto of the Parti Québécois, and has only to be implemented.

NOTES

1. Lionel Groulx, "Le Nationalisme canadien-français," Caisse populaire locale, Montreal, November 1949.
2. Paul Chamberland, "De la damnation à la liberté," in *Les Québécois* (Montreal: Editions Parti Pris, 1971), pp. 81-82.
3. Ibid., p. 87.
4. Jules-Paul Tardivel, *For My Country: An 1895 Religious and Separatist Vision of Québec Set in the Mid-Twentieth Century*, trans. Sheila Fischman (Toronto: University of Toronto Press, 1975), p. 71. The latest French edition is *Pour*

la patrie (Montreal: Les Cahiers du Québec, Editions Hurtubise-H.M.H., 1976).

5. Lionel Groulx, *Why We Are Divided* (Pamphlet reproducing a speech delivered in Montreal, November 29, 1943, under the auspices of the Ligue d'Action Nationale).

6. Sheilagh Hodgins Milner and Henry Milner, *The Decolonization of Québec,* reprinted by permission of the Canadian publishers, McClelland and Stewart, Toronto, 1976, p. 114.

7. Emile Bruchési, "L'Etat français et l'Amérique latine," *Notre avenir politique* (Montreal: Bibliothèque de l'Action Française, 1923), pp. 50-51.

8. John D. Harbron, "Influences of Spain in Latin America: 1900-1945 (M.A. thesis, University of Toronto, 1948), p. 49.

9. Excerpted from a speech to a Shell Canada management seminar, Queen's University, Kingston, July 17, 1970.

10. Ronald Sutherland, *Second Image: Comparative Studies in Québec/Canadian Literature* (Toronto: New Press, 1971), p. 112.

11. Ibid., p. 113.

12. Guy Joron, *Salaire minimum annuel $1 million! ou la course à la folie* (Montreal: Les éditions Quinze, 1976). Soon to be published in translation by General Publishing, Toronto.

3

Defining the New
Québec Nation

3

We are interested in France and the Latin countries
. . .the *résonance* of social action in Québec is
different than in the other provinces.

Roger Lemelin, editor of *La Presse*

We are convinced the progress of Mexico depends on
us and that it is founded basically in the national
market which we have the capacity to promote and
invigorate.

Gustavo Díaz Ordaz, president of Mexico
1963-1970

Québec will not be the first North American republic to
establish state capitalism based on a strong nationalist
ideology. Mexico has developed such an economy since the
1930s, with foreign ownership control and state intervention
in such key industries as energy, transportation and
communications.

The Mexican Revolution, which began in September
1910, was attended by violence and bloodshed unknown to

Canadian history and which will hopefully not attend Québec's birth as a new republic.

But the institutionalization of that revolution, beginning in the 1930s and '40s and continuing into a more modern period, bears strong parallels to the proposals of the Economic Manifesto of the Parti Québécois.

Mexican state agencies which control key resources and industries are similar to those presently in existence in Québec whose limited interventionist powers would be expanded by the Economic Manifesto.

The Mexican experience in creating a distinctive national economy next door to the United States, on which it has relied for much of its funding and technology, has not always been happy or positive.

But the system has survived with its imperfections, built-in rigidities and highly political decision-making. And it continues to attract foreign investment and multi-national corporations.

During the 1960s and '70s American, Japanese, British and European firms have competed for a place in Mexican industry, willingly accepting the participation of the state in their activities. Today about 66 percent of all economic activity in the Republic of Mexico comes under the direct or indirect control of the state.

An intense anti-Americanism (shared to a degree by Québec) is a constant stimulus to the control of American commercial and corporate activities in Mexico.

Indeed much of the political thrust of the Mexican Revolution has been directed against the historic role of the United States in Mexican domestic affairs. This relationship has included a major Mexican defeat in war against the United States and later U.S. domination of much of the republic's unstable economy in the early twentieth century.

Mexico's harsh defeat in the Mexican War of 1847 is written indelibly into the national consciousness. A third of the original Mexican republic, which had declared its independence from Spain at the beginning of the nineteenth century, was stripped from Mexico by that war. This vast territory includes the modern American states of California, Arizona, New Mexico, Colorado and Nevada.

A half-century later, the penetration of American capital and industry into the fragile Mexican economy before the outbreak of the Mexican Revolution in 1910 was extensive enough to control the resource industries of Mexican states close to the U.S. border and to influence the republic's foreign policy.

Given this kind of history, it would appear that the Mexicans have suffered greater depths of humilation, anger and resentment than the Québécois.

By comparison, the discrimination of generations of *maudit anglais* ("damned English") bosses who ordered French-Canadian workers to "speak white" (English) on the job, and closed professional positions to Québécois management, seem like a mild provocation for militant Québec nationalism.

The complaint, nevertheless, is as old as the Durham Report of 1838, which predicted the eventual disappearance of the French language from Canada. In a speech at McGill University in January 1966, an angry René Lévesque charged Montreal's "English-speaking bosses" with having a "Rhodesian-like minority frame of mind," adding that if he ever became premier he would "take over the economic life of Montreal. . .by all legitimate means. . .as soon as is humanly possible."[1]

To the modern revolutionary and nationalist, therefore, both Québec and Mexican experiences represent forms of violence against weaker societies on the defensive.

Both societies have also been exploited heavily by their own backward institutions, particularly the Roman Catholic church, which resisted the demands of intellectuals and enlightened politicians for reform.

In 1911, after the Mexican Revolution had already

begun, the Mexican Archbishop of Guadalajara pontificated: "The Christian workman should sanctify and make sublime his obedience by serving God in the person of his bosses. Poor, love your humble state and your work. Turn your gaze toward heaven. There is true wealth."[2]

While in Mexico the separation of church and state was decreed in the Constitution of 1917, in Québec the church remained extremely powerful politically until the early 1960s. In 1943 Father Richard Ares, a reactionary priest and Jesuit apologist, wrote about French-Canadians: "We are a people of peasants. Everything that takes us away from the land diminishes and weakens us as a people and encourages cross-breeding, duplicity and treason."[3]

I cite these comments from the conservative clergies of Québec and Mexico to emphasize how dramatic has been the change from a church-oriented to a technocratically managed society in both countries.

The grievance, anger and resentment which stimulated Québec and Mexican nationalism were transformed by the technicians of social change into state policies of foreign ownership control.

The Mexican Revolution, which began as a phenomenon of guerrilla warfare, banditry and destruction, was slowly consolidated in broad social reforms. Daniel Cosío Villegas, one of Mexico's most distinguished historians of this century, described the replacement of old ruling classes by new ones through the process of socializing the revolution:

> The landowner class, which held 60 to 70 percent of the country's entire wealth, disappeared. Large professional groups—the executive and political personnel, the army. . .were almost completely replaced.
>
> New social classes with a decisive political power emerged in the brand new collective owner of the

land, the industrial workers, a popular army and a
new upper class.[4]

The state began to shape the economy in the 1930s and
'40s, with the nationalization of the British and American-
owned oil industry in 1938 and the formation of large state
corporations to finance agricultural and economic growth.

The foreign companies and outside capital scared off by
the "hot" phase of the revolution, which had really ended
before petroleum nationalization in 1938, not only began
returning to Mexico but were in such demand in the years
after World War II that they put foreign-ownership control
legislation under severe strain. But it was clear that if
Mexico wished to become Latin America's first postindus-
trial nation, it would have to put aside overly rigid control
legislation based partly on old and bitter hatreds and
encourage importation of foreign technology and managerial expertise.

The present laws permitting certain levels of foreign
investment are based, therefore, on a long trial and error
process which a Québec republic will also have to face.

Québec's parallel to the Mexican era of nationalization,
stimulated by an elite of managers and technocrats who
absorbed the powers once held by the church and
reactionary politicians, did not really begin until the Quiet
Revolution in the 1960s.

Québec is now repeating the economic and social
breakthroughs already experienced in Mexico. The rapid
emergence from a rural to an urban society, and from
domination by the priest to direction by the public servant,
is marked by the feeling that what is happening in the
province has never happened before in quite the same way
in Canada.

In Mexico and Québec the most outstanding state

institutions are the government owned and managed energy corporations.

These are PEMEX (Petróleos Mexicanos or Mexican Petroleum) and Hydro-Québec, the former a primary oil and gas company (listed by the August 1977 issue of *Fortune* magazine as 70th among the 500 largest industrial corporations outside the U.S.A.), and the latter a hydro-electric power producer.

A Mexican social scientist long ago styled PEMEX ''the vertebra of the Mexican revolution.''

René Lévesque once defined Hydro-Québec as ''that great but incomplete property of the people.''[5]

PEMEX was created in March 1938 to function at the oil exploration, extraction and refining levels. The take-over of the British and American-owned oil companies was justified by the Supreme Court of Mexico on the basis of Article 27 of the Mexican Constitution of 1917, which defines the subsoil and its resources as belonging to the people of Mexico.

Hydro-Québec in its present form was established in 1963 when the privately owned power companies were bought by the province. This major step towards Québec's autonomy was spearheaded by René Lévesque as natural resources minister in the Liberal cabinet of Jean Lesage, during the first years of the Quiet Revolution.

Raymond Vernon, a distinguished American scholar of the multinational corporation, has noted: ''Every society, in the course of evolution, is likely to develop a variety of institutional forms designed to promote, control or direct the forces making for economic change. . . .In modern nations one often finds an agency charged in some general way with promoting development and with achieving some acceptable compromise of roles between public and private sectors.''[6]

Such entities as PEMEX and Hydro-Québec are defined by Professor Vernon and others as "modernizing", because not only do they control vital resource development as large public corporations, but they have also produced in each nation an elite of managers and technocrats with both professional and nationalistic commitments.

Before such powerful structures were created, the claim was that emerging societies like the Mexico of the 1940s or the Québec of the 1960s would have difficulty developing because they did not have human resources to operate and manage them.

And in both instances this was the case at the beginning. When PEMEX was formed Mexico had almost no indigenous petroleum engineers and no university courses to train them.

The first course in petroleum engineering began in 1939 at the National University of Mexico, which was then expanding to produce *técnicos* (technocrats) to steer Mexico through her period of state intervention.

A parallel institution in Québec would be the École des hautes études commerciales, whose graduates have entered the ranks of the innovators of the Quiet Revolution, the executive suites of foreign-owned branch plants, the management of Hydro-Québec and the Québec public service.

In 1970 Jacques Parizeau, in an interview for the Catholic journal *Maintenant*, discussed the role of Hydro-Québec in creating a cadre of francophone engineer-managers.

> During the course of these same years, prior to Québec power nationalization in 1962, Shawinigan Power and Light recruited very few French-Canadian engineers because it appeared it couldn't find any.
>
> The nationalization of the electricity companies has brutally changed that situation.

> And as if by a miracle, Hydro-Québec has been
> able to find the engineers of the French language it
> desired.[7]

In 1974 Rodrigue Tremblay, now the *péquiste* minister of industry, wrote in *l'Action nationale*: "It is not sufficient to modify the structure of ownership of the enterprise, but it is necessary above all to change and improve the economic environment itself."[8]

Another important state agency involved in the growth of modern Mexico is Nacional Financiera S.A. or NAFINSA, the national industrial development bank. NAFINSA was founded in 1934 to fund Mexico's lagging rural regions, but it became instead the country's major financer of industry since World War II.

Both by Mexican federal law and by custom in a highly protectionist economy, NAFINSA can intervene in any private Mexican industry or company which it decides must be "Mexicanized" in the public interest.

The 1975-76 annual report of NAFINSA states: "Nacional Financiera promotes increases in the production of basic industries. . .by the timely provision of financial resources."

NAFINSA makes loans to both public and private firms. It is involved in the government railway-car manufacturing plant and a large steel mill. In the past it has taken part as minority shareholder in such American multinationals as Celanese de Mexico. Other NAFINSA functions include tourist promotion and a role in the development of Mexican engineering consulting services for Latin America. It operates banking services at the retail level.

In 1975-76, NAFINSA reported a gross profit of about $230 million compared to $150 million the previous year, a 56-percent increase.

Québec's only parallel to NAFINSA is the small and languishing Société Générale du Financement (SGF—

General Investment Corporation), founded in 1963 at the height of the Quiet Revolution.

The purpose of the SGF is stated in its charter: "The objects of the corporation are to stimulate and facilitate the formation and development of industrial undertakings in the province so as to broaden the basis of its economic structure."

The SGF has neither an interventionist function in the Québec economy nor enough control over industry to have anything like the great economic power of NAFINSA. Also, its history to date suggests such state corporations cannot easily absorb the capital structure and managerial expertise of existing profitable companies. The SGF is presently operating at a loss.

However, Parti Québécois cultural development minister Camille Laurin says, "The entire government is convinced of the relevance of the SGF."[9]

New life for the SGF is coming in the plan for its 60-percent financial participation in the $300-million Donohue-St. Félicien Inc. paper mill (with an estimated annual capacity of 262,000 tons) in Roberval, Québec, with private paper companies taking up the rest of the share capital.

Other existing Québec state companies, such as SIDBEC, the government's primary steel mill; SOQUEM, a mining venture; SOQUIP in petroleum; and REXFOR in forestry, all point in the direction of the Mexican model of a large place for government in industry. Such companies would probably be restructured and expanded in a future Republic of Québec to the wide extent intended by the Economic Manifesto.

The similarity between contemporary Mexican laws governing joint ventures and Québec's Economic Manifesto, as yet an untried document, is revealing. It suggests that the Manifesto, if implemented by the Republic of

Québec, will represent an interventionist policy, but not one to justify the scare tactics initiated after the election of November 1976 by Anglo-Canadian industries, banks and financial institutions.

It is important to understand that foreign firms will continue to participate in the new Québec republican economy, just as they have in Mexico. Québec represents not only a large market for manufactured goods and services, but an important source of natural resources and energy.

Canada's largest province, Québec is almost three times the size of France, with a total area of almost 600,000 square miles.

In 1974 Québec's output of goods and services represented 23.7 percent of Canada's overall gross national product.

In the same year 32.3 percent of Canadian shipments of pulp and paper, Canada's major single source of foreign exchange earnings, were from Québec.

Mineral production in 1976 was 20.6 percent of the Canadian total, asbestos 100 percent of that total. Three-quarters of Canada's aluminum smelting capacity is in Québec.

Québec is also one of the world's great sources of hydro-electric power. The James Bay project, on the eastern side of James and Hudson Bays, is one of the largest power schemes in history and could cost as much as $20 billion before completion in the mid or late 1980s. Along with the existing Churchill Falls complex which Hydro-Québec bought from the British Newfoundland Corporation, this project will provide Québec industry with enough power for the rest of this century as well as allowing for export sales to both the United States and Ontario.

Even this brief outline of Québec's economic potential shows that the image of Québec as a "banana republic" has no basis in fact.

Nationalization Policies in Québec and Mexico

Although the Economic Manifesto has yet to be implemented, its Investment Code outlines the structure of foreign ownership in a future Québec republic. I would like to compare the Investment Code to a similar Mexican document, the Actividades Industriales y las Inversiones Extranjeras Directas (Industrial Activities and Direct Foreign Investments) of the Mexican Ministry of National Patrimony, which regulates the extent of foreign ownership in Mexico. Both documents were published in 1972, the Mexican chart being an update of several earlier ones published during the 1950s and '60s.

The Mexican document defines three major ownership sectors. The public sector, with 100 percent state ownership, includes hydro power, post office, telephone and telegraph, primary oil and gas exploration and production, and railways.

Some areas of the private sector are reserved for 100 percent Mexican capital, such as coastal properties, credit and related financial institutions, life insurance companies, commercial use of television and radio facilities, liquid gas and oil distribution networks, and commercial exploitation of forests.

There are areas of the private sector which admit foreign interests, but in which the major portion of share ownership and the majority of administrators must be Mexican. This classification has three subheadings: 66 percent Mexican-owned, such as special concessions in exploration of national mineral wealth; 60 percent Mexican-owned, such as secondary petrochemical activities; and the 51 percent joint-venture formula, which includes paper products, publishing, fisheries, cement, glass, basic chemicals, soft drinks, steel goods, fertilizers, and other ventures.

Not all companies and industries operating in Mexico fit into the 66, 60 or 51 percent categories. Varying

FOREIGN OWNERSHIP
REPUBLIC OF MEXICO

Industrial Activities and Direct Foreign Investments
Ministry of National Patrimony

PUBLIC SECTOR

(100% state ownership)

- primary oil and gas, including refining
- hydro power
- post office
- railways

PRIVATE SECTOR

100% Mexican capital

- coastal property
- credit, insurance, finance and investment companies
- forestry
- radio and television
- bus transport on federal highways

66% Mexican capital	60% Mexican capital	51% Mexican capital
- mineral explorations - concessions in mineral reserves#	- secondary petroleum industries	- book publishing - fisheries - film production - glass - fertilizer - cement - plastics - aluminum - bottled soft drinks - maritime transport - paper products (a selected list)

\# The Mexican Mining Law of 1960 requires all Mexican mining properties to be Mexican-owned (private or public sector) by 1981.

FOREIGN OWNERSHIP
REPUBLIC OF QUÉBEC

Investment Code
Parti Québécois Economic Manifesto*

PUBLIC SECTOR

(100% state ownership)

- hydro power
- asbestos†
- post office
- railways and seaway
- one or two chartered banks (to be nationalized)

PRIVATE SECTOR

100% Québec capital

- media, TV, radio and newspapers
- insurance firms and trust companies
- retail distribution of energy products, such as heating oil

75% Québec capital	51% Québec capital
- banks	- steel
	- electrical products
	- communications equipment

---

* *La prochaine étape. . .quand nous serons vraiment chez nous* (Montreal, Editions Parti Québécois, 1972).

† The Economic Manifesto proposes a consortium of private Québec-owned firms to take control of the asbestos industry. However, Premier Lévesque, following the November 1976 election, promised the industry would be nationalized.

proportions of foreign ownership may be negotiated between a company and the Mexican government, and 100 percent foreign ownership is allowed in certain instances (see footnote 12).

In addition to the foreign ownership sectors detailed on the chart, a separate Mexican Mining Law, passed in 1960 during the nationalistic presidency of Adolfo López Mateos, calls for Mexicanization of the entire mining industry by 1980.

Initial reaction to the Mexican Mining Law among foreign-owned mining interests was that it represented a form of deferred but still direct expropriation. What has happened in most instances is that foreign mining firms have settled for minority ownership pending complete Mexican control in 1980, and have benefited from the provisions that Mexican-controlled mining firms receive an automatic 50 percent rebate on most production and export taxes.

These and other Mexican laws and decrees restricting foreign control have their juridical basis in the Constitution of 1917 (such as Article 27 which defines the subsoil of Mexico as belonging to the people).

As a result of the foreign-ownership laws and policy statements over the period from 1940 to 1975, about 60 percent of Mexican industries and services are government owned, government operated or government financed.

The Investment Code of the Economic Manifesto is not as specific as the Mexican document, since it has not yet become legislation. However, it proposes a division of the economy into sectors quite similar to the ones outlined in the Mexican chart.

The public sector would include such industries as hydro power, asbestos (at least according to René Lévesque), postal services, railways and the seaway, and probably one or two of the chartered banks which would be nationalized.

The private sector would have several subsections. Companies which would eventually come under 100 percent

Québec ownership would include the media industry—TV, radio, newspaper, book and magazine publishing. The 75 percent Québec ownership category would include banks that were not nationalized. A third category would be 51 percent Québec ownership, which would include electrical and communications equipment companies such as Northern Electric, RCA Victor and General Electric.

In addition, foreign control would be permitted in certain industries in which the importation of foreign technology was necessary.

Québec possesses other instruments for control and direction of the economy besides the Investment Code. They are clearly outlined with their proposed functions in the original Economic Manifesto:

Caisse de dépôt et placement (Québec Deposit and Investment Fund). This agency, which invests the Québec Pension Plan, could be used to buy up newly issued stock of local companies whose ownership must be placed under Québec control, or to invest in newly formed joint ventures.

To accomplish these goals, it would need substantially more funds from the Québec Pension Plan (QPP). But financial analysts doubt that the Québec Pension Fund as presently constructed could supply the funds needed for extensive buying-out of foreign industry in Québec.

The QPP's formula for employer and employee contributions is based on the Canada Pension Plan and everyone must participate in it. But the QPP is no longer new, and an increasing number of its contributors are reaching retirement age when they will start to draw on the plan.

To meet future demands of the caisse de dépôt et placement, the QPP must do two things: increase the present contribution formula, and persuade the unions that their employees should permit the caisse de dépôt et placement to manage their funds. Union leaders, even those sympathetic to other Parti Québécois goals for extending Québec control over foreign-owned branch plants, have expressed strong disagreement with this latter proposal.

Caisses populaires. It would be necessary to persuade not only the managers, but the hundreds of thousands of small Québec investors in these unique credit unions, to invest their funds in the future take-over of something as gigantic as a chartered bank, which is one of the uses for the caisses populaires proposed in the Economic Manifesto.

Meanwhile the caisses populaires are performing very well. In 1976 their assets increased more than $1 billion, from $4.86 billion in 1975 to $5.89 billion in 1976.

Mr. Alfred Rouleau, president of the Fédération des Caisses Populaires, has hinted at loyalty to the present Québec government in his statements on the future policy of his organization. On March 9, 1977 he told the annual meeting in Québec City that the caisses populaires will be "one of the institutions Québec citizens can count on in their collective efforts."

Mr. Rouleau also rejected proposed amendments to the federal Bank Act (which is under review at the end of 1977) which would require the caisses populaires to maintain reserves with the central Bank of Canada. His statement, "We have affirmed our wish to remain subject to one jurisdiction, that being the provincial jurisdiction,"[10] indicates that the caisses populaires may be preparing for the role proposed for them by the Economic Manifesto.

Bank control legislation. Though *péquiste* spokesmen denied vigorously after the November 1976 election that this part of the Economic Manifesto would ever be implemented, the new finance minister was later to speak differently. Jacques Parizeau, the major architect of the Manifesto, told a business conference in Toronto on April 25, 1977: "The parent bank, with its head office in Toronto, will not hold more than 10 percent of the shares of its offspring in Montreal, and. . .nonresidents will not be allowed to hold more than a quarter of the capital stock of a Québec bank.''[11]

Under the Bank Act, all Canadian chartered banks must have their head offices in Canada. When Québec separates she will lose the head offices of the banks presently located in Montreal, such as the Royal Bank and Bank of Montreal, with the resulting loss of business for the many supplier companies.

Despite the wild conjectures by English-Canadian business firms as to how many companies would flee the province, the threats of the chartered banks to leave Québec were based as much on the requirements of the federal Bank Act as on their fear of control legislation that would be imposed if Québec became independent.

Socìéte de réorganisation industrielle (Industrial Reorganization Corporation). The Economic Manifesto envisions a large state investment corporation not unlike Mexico's Nacional Financiera, ''charged by the state with the direction of a certain number of major participants who dominate the transformation of the industrial structure.'' As with NAFINSA, this could mean partial financing of selected industries, or complete take-over by majority purchase of their capital stock. In forming the Industrial Reorganization Corporation, the government of Québec will already have a guideline in the SGF, which was described earlier in this chapter.

The most severe cultural instrument of the new Québec republic will be the French Language Charter or Bill 101, which makes French the official language of Québec.

Bill 101 replaces the earlier Bill 22, which was introduced by the Liberal government of Robert Bourassa. The new bill will have a watchdog agency, the *Commission de surveillance*, which will have greater powers than the earlier *Régie de la langue française*, to enforce the French-only law.

It is interesting that the cultural instrument for the new Québec should be the first major piece of legislation passed by the National Assembly controlled by the Parti Québécois.

The warnings that a Republic of Québec will mean unbridled socialism have come mainly from Montreal-based corporations dominated by English-Canadian senior management and shareholders who have usually had their own way in Québec's business community. A Québec republic will become so state-oriented, they predict, that the private sector, entrepreneurship and vital foreign investment will all wither on the vine.

Yet in Mexico, with all its foreign-control legislation, three major areas of private endeavor continue to flourish. These are the foreign-owned branch plant, the locally controlled conglomerate or venture capital company, and the native entrepreneur.

Much of the success of each has depended on its ability and willingness to make the state a partner in its activities. Cooperation with the state is required by law in the case of the branch plant, but is less formal where the conglomerate and the entrepreneur are concerned. The state, through its various agencies (for example Nacional Financiera), can be a partner in the conglomerate or a customer for the entrepreneur.

And while the national market of a developing country inhibits the foreign-owned branch plant, making it a minority partner, this does not reduce its market prospects or its profits. In fact American and European multinational corporations have increased their overseas sales as a percentage of their total sales during the late 1960s and early '70s.

Let us investigate a major American company with joint venture operations in the Mexican economy.

The Du Pont Company first entered Mexico with a wholly owned firm manufacturing paints, agricultural chemicals and explosives. Technically this was not a violation of long-existing Mexican foreign control legislation, because some of the products used feedstocks purchased from PEMEX, the state-owned oil corporation, and under Mexican law secondary industries in the petrochemical field may be wholly owned in the private sector by foreigners.

Du Pont's further expansion into Mexico began in the late 1950s with a plan to build the country's only titanium plant near the government's petrochemical complex at Tampico on the Gulf of Mexico.

Since it was to be a one-of-a-kind new manufacturing facility, and would not compete with any existing Mexican plant, Du Pont hoped to build a 100-percent company-owned plant. But this was during the strongly nationalistic administration of President Adolfo López Mateos, and Du Pont had to settle for a joint venture with the 51-percent controlling interest in the titanium plant held by the Banco de Comercio.

During the 1960s Du Pont penetrated further into the Mexican chemical field, and by 1977 its role in the Mexican chemical industry, in a country with strong control measures over foreign-owned multinationals, was much larger than its role in Québec.

In spite of tough Mexicanization laws, E.I. Du Pont de Nemours still has four wholly owned Mexican operations as well as six joint ventures.[12]

By comparison, all of Du Pont's Canadian and Québec plants are wholly owned by Du Pont of Canada, which in turn is wholly owned by the parent company in Wilmington, Delaware.

The comments made in 1969 by F. B. Loretta, former head of Du Pont's Mexican operations, are in marked contrast to the current panic tactics employed by business about the future role of this kind of large company in Québec:

> I would be less than honest if I did not state that generally Du Pont would prefer to own 100 percent of a foreign subsidiary and certainly we prefer owning a majority of a venture rather than a minority.
>
> . . .I have mentioned the disadvantages from our standpoint of joint ventures such as restricted freedom of action, concern over security of know-how, less earnings. . . .
>
> Our experience has shown that most of these can be handled and consequently are more imaginary than real.[13]

Foreign-owned branch plants in the Québec republic will be structured and managed on the basis of their parent companies' substantial prior experience with joint ventures and foreign ownership laws in Mexico, Spain, Indonesia, Venezuela, etc.

What is critical to all of them is not necessarily the actual event of independence, but rather the extent to which a Québec republican government commits itself to foreign control laws and how well it manages them.

A second area of private endeavor which has been important to Mexico and could also be applied to a future Québec economy is the locally owned conglomerate.

These conglomerates have been formed by nationalistic Mexican entrepreneurs with personal connections to the Mexican government as well as international industry and finance. They are essentially partnerships of funds, technology and management which benefit several industries at one time, all within the restrictive laws requiring that such firms be Mexican-controlled.

One example is Intercontinental S.A., formed in the late 1950s by Mexican multi-millionaire Bruno Pagliai, who organized partners and cash resources involving shipbuilding, aluminum smelting, oil drilling equipment and steel products.

In Intercontinental's original capitalization package 35 percent of the shares were held by the conglomerate, 16 percent by other Mexican investors, 35 percent by the Aluminum Company of America (Alcoa) and 14 percent by American & Foreign Power (which was nationalized in 1960).

Intercontinental's own stock was in turn sold to foreign as well as Mexican concerns, including Krupp and Siemens (West Germany), Techint (Italy), Syndicat Belge d'Entreprise (Belgium) and First California Co. (U.S.A.)

This kind of conglomerate, which does not control a major source of capital or technology but instead involves perhaps a dozen foreign sources of funds and expertise, has greater potential for a Québec republic's diversification needs than would a total reliance on the operations of foreign concerns resistant by nature to foreign ownership control laws.

A third element in the economic development of a national market (indeed of any economy) is the entrepreneur.

The Mexican entrepreneur has the same motivation to amass wealth and build business empires as have entrepreneurs anywhere else, but at the same time he is strongly nationalistic in pursuit of private goals.

An American academic specializing in Latin American entrepreneurship writes this of the Mexican entrepreneur:

> Not a few economists have asserted that the Mexican entrepreneur refrains from making long-term investments and concentrates on near liquidity of investment activities. . . .
> . . .Such a contention is simply not substantiated by Mexican entrepreneurship. They have promoted

and managed scores of textile mills, forty pulp and paper mills, twenty cement plants, ten caustic soda plants, and over 100 shoe factories. [14]

In other words, an entrepreneurial class was not only permitted to develop in Mexico but has played an important role in the economy, organizing management and capital resources to form locally owned companies and to serve as representatives for foreign firms.

In the past the Mexican entrepreneurial potential was often inhibited by the dominance and the superior skills of foreigners. Often the Mexican engineer, accountant or economist would work for the multinational rather than strike out on his own. Recently this is less frequently the case.

This parallels entrepreneurial patterns in Québec, where a portion of the professional and managerial talent is absorbed by the foreign-owned branch plants. Québec's independence could inspire entrepreneurs to branch out on their own, sharing as they would the pride of nation which is a definable element of the modern Mexican entrepreneur.

Hazards of a National Market

The negative aspects of creating a national market and an economy restricted by nationalization laws should not be overlooked in surveying the Mexican experience.

Harsh laws limiting the participation of foreign-owned entities who bring with them investment funds and fresh ideas, import substitution legislation requiring costly local manufacture of consumer goods, and the bureaucratic chaos of administering such an economy—all have been part of Mexican economic nationalism.

Miguel Wionczek, a leading economist with the Centro Nacional de Productividad (National Productivity Centre), a Mexican government supported institute, has remained pessimistic about the overall success of the revolutionary experience. He claims that unequal distribution of wealth in Mexico has hardly changed in twenty-five years.

The manufacture of import substitutions under heavy tariffs which restrict competitive foreign imports entering the Mexican market has several drawbacks, says Wionczek. Industrialists have been able to hide excess profits behind protection mechanisms, and diversification of Mexican-made products has been increasingly difficult because of the monopoly they enjoy.

The long-standing Ministry of National Patrimony regulations governing joint venture arrangements do not always guarantee that the majority of shareholders are Mexican citizens or that companies are Mexican-owned. There are means, encouraged by the system itself, whereby Mexican participants in a new enterprise are in effect funded by outside interests through bank loans, complex foreign credit arrangements or laundered funds, so that a company critical to a phase of Mexican economic development can still be under foreign control.

Nationalization or partial take-over procedures are also costly, not only in terms of the public funds needed to carry them out, but in the loss of economic momentum and good management which they entail.

An extreme-left regime will greatly stimulate nationalization. The recently terminated administration of Luís Echeverría (1970-1977) gave Mexico a strong Third World political thrust and dealt harshly with foreign ownership and with Mexico's need for imported technical skills. Mexico's drop in exports, the administration's open threats against foreign branch plants, and Echeverría's intense anti-Americanism all contributed to two severe devaluations of the Mexican peso, which had not been devalued since 1954.[15]

The lesson to be learned from this is that the strength of a future Québec currency will depend partly on the rigidity with which foreign ownership regulations are implemented. There must be guarantees that foreign companies will be able to function profitably within the new republican economy and that they will be permitted to expatriate a portion of their earnings.

Yet even in a highly nationalistic economy, a well-run corporation will always attract investors. Thus it is that while both Québec and Mexico have record high unemployment, a downturn in productivity and a decline in exports, their largest state-run energy corporations (Hydro-Québec and PEMEX) continue to win confidence from the New York money markets.

The emerging Québec republic will probably be initially considered a political risk by the international financial institutions, as was Mexico in the 1940s. But if her future political leadership is stable, and if she avoids a rush to Third-World-style economics, Québec will survive her political decision to become a republic.

A Foreign Policy for the New Republic

Before the Parti Québécois swept into power in November 1976, Québec had already begun to make its own foreign policy in what Professor Louis Sabourin calls "a distinctive Québec presence and behavior on the world scene."[16]

This was manifested in Québec's renewed cordiality during the 1960s with France, mother country of her culture and language, and in new ties with the other French-speaking nations of the world.

Where France and Québec had ignored each other during the 1950s when the Union Nationale political machine held power, the Quiet Revolution and the emergence from it of a class of technocrats created a need for liaison with the managers of the *planification économique*, the famous French experiment in central planning.

Moreover, several of the important political leaders and

public servants in Québec City during the early 1960s had been educated in French schools and universities.

The Algerian war of independence from France in the early 1960s had an influence at another level in Québec political life.

The extremist wings within the newly emerging separatist parties denounced the Quiet Revolution as a mere reshuffling of the existing power bases from the priests and patronage-hungry politicians to the secular managers and rising business elites. They visualized a war for the liberation of Québec like that waged and ultimately won by the FLN (Front de Libération Nationale) in Algeria.

Thus, while the working papers of France's *planification économique* on housing, social reform and economic planning had become gospel to the new cadres of innovative public servants in Québec City, Frantz Fanon's *Wretched of the Earth*, written partly in Algiers during the revolutionary conflict, was a bible for Québec's extremists.

France, too, responded to the social and political changes in Québec, where before she had forgotten the once passive residue of herself on the distant St. Lawrence River.

Gaullist France of the mid and late 1960s looked to Québec partly as an abandoned diadem of a bygone imperial era. France had substituted an African empire for the vast American one lost in 1763, but was compelled to reassess her position in the Francophone world as a result of her defeat in the Algerian war and the emergence of independent black African nations from the French African colonies.

At the same time, French capitalists and multi-national companies, especially in the oil and gas industries, saw Québec and Canada as new markets for their investment and skills to take the place of Algeria, where the oil and gas sectors had been nationalized.

The renewed friendship between France and Québec did not begin with the impertinent and ungracious shout of

"Vive le Québec libre" by General de Gaulle in Montreal during Expo '67.

Québec's "awakening" was made known in France in 1961, when Premier Jean Lesage went to Paris to open the $350,000 Maison du Québec and was received by de Gaulle with as much panoply as Canadian prime ministers on state visits.

In October 1963 André Malraux, intellectual giant and de Gaulle's minister of state for cultural affairs, visited Québec with an entourage of 130 French business executives and leaders of the arts. He spoke encouraging words for a Québec newly launched on its own era: "I say to you, French Canadians, that we will build tomorrow's civilization together."[17]

A new battleground in Canadian federal-provincial relations was created by Québec's efforts at parity with already independent Francophone African nations during the late 1960s.

The first of these was the "Gabon Incident," which resulted from the attendance of Québec education minister Jean-Guy Cardinal at a conference of education ministers from French-speaking countries. Friction was caused by Mr. Cardinal's personal efforts to help organize the African conferences without first consulting the Department of External Affairs, and by the fact that his invitation from the Gabon Republic went directly to Québec City and not Ottawa.

Commenting on the Gabon affair, Bernard Kaplan, Paris correspondent for the *Montreal Star*, wrote on January 11, 1968: "For the first time, Québec will participate as the peer of sovereign states and without reference to Ottawa in an international meeting at the ministerial level."[18]

The Gabon incident was taken seriously enough by the Canadian government that Mr. Trudeau suspended diplomatic relations with the new African republic. It also prompted the federal government to produce a white paper on protocol in these matters. Entitled *Federalism and International Relations*, it said: "In official dealings with other countries, that is to say in the conduct of foreign relations in the strict sense of that term, only the Federal Government is empowered to act on behalf of Canada."[19]

Ivan Head, before he was appointed principal adviser on foreign policy to the prime minister in 1968, made a most interesting comment about the implications of the Gabon affair for a Québec effort at separate identification in international conferences. Speaking on the former CBC commentary program "Viewpoint," Mr. Head suggested that the Gabon invitation "was a formal act of recognition of the international independence of Québec, of the same effect as if Gabon had announced to the world that it now regards Québec as a separate, independent state not forming part of Canada." Referring to the Halibut Treaty of 1923, which Canada signed separately from Britain to encourage U.S. recognition of its nation status, Mr. Head continued: "Québec may well achieve international independence in precisely the same fashion that Canada itself employed forty-five years ago."[20]

The conflict was renewed in January 1969 when another education conference of Francophone nations was held in Kinshasa, capital of the Congo (later to be called Zaïre). It resulted in correspondence between Prime Minister Trudeau and Québec Premier Jean-Jacques Bertrand (who was Union Nationale and not a separatist) over an acceptable formula for Québec's continued role in conferences of the French-speaking world.

"In the event of a possible vote at the conference, Canada including Québec will have only one vote," Mr. Trudeau informed Bertrand. "If the members of the delegation cannot reach an agreement, Canada will abstain."[21]

Later that month, a visit to Paris by Québec education minister Jean-Guy Cardinal on behalf of ailing Premier Bertrand was accorded the pomp usually reserved for a head

QUÉBEC

ATLANTIC
OCEAN

HAITI

MEXICO

VENEZUELA
GUYANE

PACIFIC
OCEAN

BRAZIL

||||||||| FRENCH-SPEAKING

‒ ‒ ‒ ‒ SPANISH-SPEAKING

CHILE

· · · · · PORTUGUESE-
         SPEAKING

ARGENTINA

A COMPARATIVE SELECTION OF LATIN AMERICAN REPUBLICS OF
THE 1980s

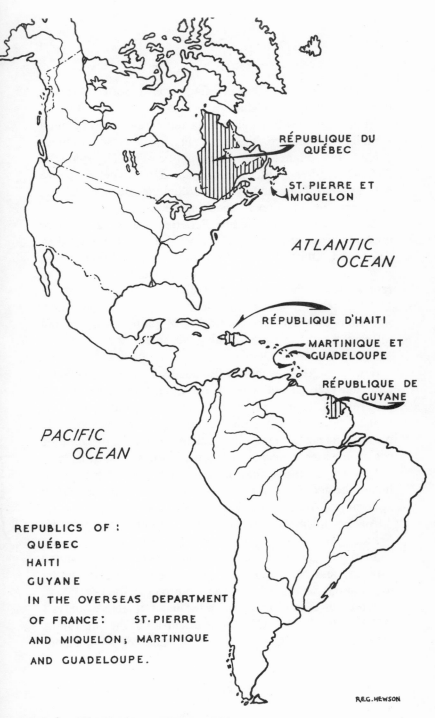

RÉPUBLIQUE DU
QUÉBEC

ST. PIERRE ET
MIQUELON

ATLANTIC
OCEAN

RÉPUBLIQUE D'HAITI

MARTINIQUE ET
GUADELOUPE

RÉPUBLIQUE DE
GUYANE

PACIFIC
OCEAN

REPUBLICS OF:
QUÉBEC
HAITI
GUYANE
IN THE OVERSEAS DEPARTMENT
OF FRANCE: ST. PIERRE
AND MIQUELON; MARTINIQUE
AND GUADELOUPE.

R.E.G. HEWSON

FRENCH AMERICA OF THE 1980s

of state, and the Québec flag was reportedly given precedence over the Canadian.

In February 1969, Québec City and Ottawa worked out a formula for joint participation in meetings at Niamey, capital of the French-speaking Republic of the Niger, on the formation of an international agency to promote the *francophonie* community by coordinating aid and cultural exchanges among French-speaking nations.

Secretary of State Gérard Pelletier was to go to that conference as the one and only head of the Canadian delegation. But the federal government agreed that among the provinces in attendance only Québec would be represented at the ministerial levels.

A more serious recent development has been the intrusions on Canadian sovereignty by junior ministers and influential civil servants of the government of France.

These began in October 1969 with the indiscreet but carefully staged speeches in Canada by Jean de Lipkowski, an under secretary of state for foreign affairs in the French government. Lipkowski's public remarks about the duty of France to aid Québec in its 200-year-old struggle ''to preserve its national identity'' called for a response from the prime minister, who put his views in the strongest terms.

Charges in the Canadian press throughout the 1970s linked the activities of *agents provocateurs* from the French government to the rising Parti Québécois.

An article in the *Oshawa Times* reported promises by French government agents in Canada that France would support the cause of Québec independence in the United Nations, and of Québec as a separate state in her future negotiations with the European Common Market.[22]

Professor Louis Sabourin, in the most objective analysis to date of the Québec City-Ottawa scuffles of the late 1960s, viewed them as ''more often. . .a result of spontaneous behavior. . .than through predetermined, long-standing plans.''[23]

His calmer reasoning could be explained by the fact that his essay was published in an official journal of the Department of External Affairs. But, whether Québec's actions were spontaneous or planned, the fact remains that a foreign policy for the future nation was already in the making during the late 1960s while Québec was still a province.

The Québec ministry of inter-governmental affairs under Mr. Claude Morin (who was deputy minister during the late 1960s) is being groomed for its future role as foreign ministry of the Republic of Québec. Mr. Morin's reception during his Paris visit of April-May 1977 indicates that support will come easily from France for Québec's entry into various international organizations.

Whether the Republic of Québec will ultimately be a contributing or a borrowing nation in the international banking agencies will depend largely on the state of her economy and the amount of her external debt at the time of independence.

The strength of her resources base, the extent of her industrial development and her large gross national product suggest Québec will join the World Bank and perhaps the Inter-American Development Bank (organized in 1961 by the major Latin American republics) as well.

Québec's entry into the World Bank would probably mean an almost immediate request for a multi-billion-dollar "stand-by" loan, of the kind made to Britain during the 1970s, to assist an economy cut off from the rest of Canada.

Québec will need such a loan to replace revenues from terminated federal-provincial tax-sharing agreements and federal regional development grants; and for the purchase of Québec's portion of federal crown corporations such as Air

Canada, the St. Lawrence Seaway Authority, the post office, and railway facilities. Also, Québec will no longer have the federal subsidies of recent years to help her meet the increasing cost of the foreign oil which she will continue to import in large quantities.

Canada's support for the entry of the Republic of Québec into the World Bank could be ironic. Any loans approved for the new republic, in which Canada would have to concur as a World Bank member, would be used by Québec for somewhat the same purposes as the funds once obtained from the federal-provincial tax-sharing agreements, which have been attacked as one of the causes of Québec's subservience to Ottawa.

The policy of the Québec republic on NATO, the United Nations, and NORAD (North American Air Defense Agreement) is already clearly discernible before independence. Position papers and resolutions presented at annual Parti Québécois conferences have strongly opposed Québec's participation as a new state in military alliances of any kind.

This further suggests that a future Québec military establishment, depending to what extent it is formed of Francophone personnel from the Canadian Armed Forces and shared military equipment (the latter a totally unlikely prospect), would be geared to a passive role in the hemisphere, perhaps acting as nothing more than a national guard.

The fact that a separate Québec will opt out of NORAD should not cause friction with the Pentagon, since the protective umbrella of defense over North America will still include Québec air space. In other words, Québec's self-proclaimed neutrality (like that of Mexico) will not hinder North American air defense strategy if the United States is compelled to defend herself against a Soviet attack.

In the United Nations, the Republic of Québec as a member country will assume a more deterministic role in controversial world situations than Canada has done. If such a crisis as the two Chinas were to arise again, Québec would probably not engage in the lengthy equivocation which marked Canada's official position between 1950 and her final recognition of the People's Republic of China in October 1970.

In the decades-old Arab-Israeli crisis, which one can only assume will still be active when Québec takes her seat in the U.N., Québec's support for Israel could not be taken for granted. If Québec were to become a militant Third World nation, she would probably support such contentious causes as the Palestinian homeland. And if so, she would find herself at loggerheads with Canadian positions in the U.N.

After France, Québec would probably be the major contributor of technical expertise and cultural assistance to the Francophone Third World in Africa, Oceania and Latin America. This would include the People's Republic of Vietnam, the struggling Asian Communist state with which a Québec republic would share a French colonial heritage as well as leftist political ideologies.

Québec's relations with her fellow Latin American republics should develop an intimacy which was difficult between pre-secessionist Canada and Latin America. French-Canadian politicians and intellectuals have been distinctly aware of social changes in other Latin societies and have recommended that Canada join the Pan American Union and the successor Organization of American States. Canada appointed a Permanent Observer to the OAS in 1972, but has taken no further steps towards full membership.[24] Québec, on the other hand, will likely wish to become a full OAS member after independence.

The interest of Mexico in the Québec experience with nationhood would be self-evident. Québec's relations with Venezuela as a continuing major source of petroleum would also be intimate, since the new republic would not benefit from domestic pricing arrangements when new petroleum resources are found in Arctic offshore oil explorations and the Athabasca tar sands.

The appearance in Québec City of economic and technical missions from Venezuela, Brazil, and Mexico is not an unlikely prospect if Québec moves to control her natural resources through state corporations. This tendency towards cooperation among state companies already exists in Latin American countries, with technology and product-sharing agreements between PEMEX, Mexico's state oil agency, and PETROBRAS, the Brazilian equivalent established during the 1970s.

As early as 1961, a brief to the Parent Provincial Royal Commission on Education recommended that Québec's cultural affairs ministry have separate departments for Latin America and Latin Europe, and that delegations be opened in all the major capitals of the Latin world. An independent Québec will likely sponsor cultural mission exchanges and perhaps establish several *Maisons québécoises* in the larger Latin American republics.

A major dilemma facing all developing Latin societies is that most of the answers to vital technical questions must still be found in an Anglo-Saxon world of industry and management which scorns emotion, tradition and historical circumstance in the decision-making process. Québec will be forced to combine pragmatic management with highly emotional ideological goals, and in this she will be closer to the Latin republics of the Western Hemisphere than to the European socialist models.

One should not anticipate a rush to abandon Québec by U.S. and foreign-owned companies who chose the large and lucrative Québec market in the first place because of its sophisticated consumer responses to their products and services and its abundance of resources.

U.S. Ambassador Thomas Enders has stated publicly that American-owned firms in Québec will find it easier to accept the tough requirement that companies use French in their head offices than English-Canadian firms are prepared to do. "The American firms may not be affected by psychological factors," he said in a Montreal speech.[25]

Many of the U.S. multi-national firms in Québec also do business with much more deeply committed socialist and authoritarian systems than Québec intends to become, at least as indicated by the Economic Manifesto.

The continuation of American confidence in Québec is indicated by the fact that on July 18, 1977, the American weekly newsmagazine *U.S. News and World Report* said that the General Motors of Canada assembly plant at Ste. Thérèse, Québec, is to receive a $36-million extension with an estimated 15-percent growth in the intermediate-size cars produced for the North American market.

American management methods will continue to predominate in the manufacturing sectors where U.S. branch plants now control Québec industries.

The public administration methods of Montreal's École des hautes études commerciales and Paris's *planification économique* will be used by Québec's republican government, the state enterprises and government-dominated joint ventures.

It is unlikely that the U.S.-owned branch plants in Québec (with an investment as large as American investments in all of Latin America) will have any reason to encourage the intervention of the U.S. State Department or CIA-style manipulation of the kind that helped bring down the Marxist Allende government in Chile.

"Destabilization" is undoubtedly in the minds of René Lévesque and company. The present Parti Québécois government does not appear to have an Allende- or Manley-style statist economy in mind, but if a post-Lévesque government is militant and revolutionary enough, destabilization becomes a clear possibility.

Québec has not only the will but also the natural and

human resources to survive as a nation. Only unforeseen events could inhibit her orderly emergence as the thirty-first independent nation in the Western Hemisphere.

Threats of intervention from Ottawa or the United States could provoke a coalition of extremist groups and militant trade unions within Québec itself. The removal of René Lévesque, with his commitment to the peaceful evolution and orderly development of the Québec republic, would present the new nation with frightening uncertainties.

NOTES

1. Claude Arpin, "How René Lévesque would run the new Québec," *Toronto Telegram*, May 22, 1971.
2. Lewis Hanke, *Mexico and the Caribbean: Modern Latin America in Ferment*, vol. 1 (New York: Van Nostrand Reinhold, 1967), p. 99.
3. Milner and Milner, *Decolonization of Québec*.
4. Daniel Cosío Villegas, *Changes in Latin America: The Mexican and Cuban Revolutions* (Lincoln: University of Nebraska Press, 1961), p. 13.
5. Sauriol, *Nationalization of Electric Power*, p. 10.
6. Raymond Vernon, ed., *Public Policy and Private Enterprise in Mexico* (Cambridge: Harvard University Press, 1964), p. 193.
7. *Maintenant*, no. 93 (February 1970), p. 43.
   Mr. Parizeau is not entirely correct in his assumption with regard to the expansion of professional groups in Québec. A classic study on the career choices of graduates from the *collèges classiques* of Québec in the years immediately after World War II was made in the late 1960s by Québec sociologist Jean Charles Falardeau.
   Of 9,304 students who graduated from the *collèges classiques* between 1939 and 1950, 37 percent chose medicine, 11 percent engineering, 7 percent law, 5 percent commerce and only 4 percent applied science. In other words, in the immediate postwar era there was a very real shortage of graduates in engineering and applied sciences. Edward Corbett, *Québec Confronts Canada* (Baltimore, Johns Hopkins Press, 1967), pp. 188-9.

8. Rodrigue Tremblay, "Les Québécois et leur économie," *L'Action nationale* 64, no. 10 (June 1975), p. 809.

9. "Lévesque's Quest for a Nation," special report in *Financial Post*, June 11, 1977, pp. 14-15.
   On the early SGF see the French press release "Le Financement des entreprises dans la Province du Québec," Gérard Filion, director general of the SGF, Canadian Management Centre, Montreal, February 3-4, 1965.

10. "Assets rise $1 billion for caisses populaires," *Globe and Mail*, March 9, 1977.

11. "Parizeau assesses future relations of a separated Québec," *Globe and Mail*, April 26, 1977.

12. In 1977 Du Pont had the following wholly owned and joint-venture operations in Mexico. Du Pont (plastics imported from the U.S.A.), Colorquím (pigments), La-Domincia (fluorspar), Laboratorios Endo de México (analgesics), are 100-percent owned by the U.S. parent company.
    Tetraétilo de México (gasoline additives) and Pigmentos y Productos Químicos are both 49-percent foreign owned; Nylon de México 40 percent; Química Fluor 33 percent; Halocarburos (freon gas) 25 percent; and Fomento Minero (hydrofluoric acid) 17-percent foreign owned. Public Relations Department, Du Pont, Wilmington, Delaware.

13. I.A. Litvak and C.J. Maule, "Foreign Investment in Mexico: Some Lessons for Canada," *Behind the Headlines*, Canadian Institute of International Affairs, vol. 30, nos. 5-6 (July 1971), pp. 10-11.
    See also John D. Harbron, "Pemex at Twenty-Five," *Fortune*, August 1963, pp. 87-88; an account of the activities of foreign-owned petrochemical companies in Mexico during the early 1960s and their relations with the state oil corporation.

14. Frank Brandenburg, "The Case of Mexico: A Contribution to the Theory of Entrepreneurship and Economic Development," *Inter-American Economic Affairs*, Washington, D.C., vol. 16, no. 3 (Winter 1962), p. 23.

15. Many analyses of the Mexican peso devaluation appeared in North American business publications. See "The Sobering Effect of Two Devaluations," *Business Week*, September 3, 1976.

16. Louis Sabourin, "Québec's international activity rests on an

idea of competence," *International Perspectives*, Department of External Affairs, Ottawa, March-April 1977, p. 3.

17. *Time*, October 18, 1963.
18. "The Education of Gabon," *Canadian Annual Review*, 1968, ed. John T. Saywell (Toronto: University of Toronto Press), p. 223.
19. Ibid.
20. Ibid., p. 226.
21. "Canada, Québec and France," *Canadian Annual Review*, 1969, p. 194.
22. "De Gaulle men reported active here," *Oshawa Times*, December 13, 1976.
23. Sabourin, op. cit.
24. On September 7, 1977, Prime Minister Trudeau took part in the historic signing of the Panama Canal Treaties in the Washington, D.C. headquarters of the OAS, as a guest of that organization. However, after the event Trudeau said that Canada would not join the OAS at present.
25. Canadian Press report on speech of U.S. Ambassador Thomas Enders, Montreal, April 4, 1977.

4

Republic of Québec:
A Third-World Alternative

4

Every young Québécois who is twenty years old theoretically carries a bomb under his arm.

Claude Jasmin, *Ethel
and the Terrorist*

We will have no history. . .until the moment we begin revolutionary war.

Hubert Aquin, *Prochain
épisode*

There is a fearful alternative to the social democracy envisioned by René Lévesque and the urbane technocrats in his cabinet.

That is a radicalized Québec republic ruled by a post-Lévesque demagogue and a coalition of the highly politicized trade unions, with their public pledge to "break the system," the growing population of the youthful unemployed, and the extreme left of the Parti Québécois.

This kind of union of extreme nationalist and anti-capitalist forces would not be new in our hemisphere. Given the right kind of charismatic leader, the Argentine experience of Peronism could be transferred from the Southern to the Northern Hemisphere.

During the late 1940s and early '50s, Juan Domingo Perón and his dynamic wife Evita joined restless social forces in an ideological alliance of extreme nationalism and intense anti-Americanism.

Argentina in the 1950s was going through a slow transition not unlike that of Québec in the 1960s. The large and politically powerful Argentine Confederación General de Trabajadores (CGT, General Confederation of Workers) was as militantly nationalistic and strongly antiforeign as is the Confederation of National Trade Unions (CNTU) in modern Québec.

Perón used the CGT as the major element in his union of labor, radical students, large sectors of the army, and disenfranchised bourgeoisie unhappy with the slow changes in Argentine society. He called it an alliance of *los descamisados* ("the shirtless ones").[1]

That alliance, both during the mid-1950s and in altered form during the second *peronista* episode of 1973-76, set class against class, launched Argentina on disastrous programs of import substitution by purposefully ignoring essential foreign technology, and made enemies of big trading partners like Britain and the U.S.A.

The originally conservative Québec labor syndicates that came together in 1922 to form the Confédération des Travailleurs Catholiques du Canada (Canadian and Catholic Confederation of Labour, CCCL) would continue to respond more sharply to the wide ideological shifts in Québec than any other institution or group—the church, intellectuals or provincial governments.

The CCCL of the prewar years was committed to the containment of "outside materialistic forces" from the American international unions, because they represented a threat to still-strong Catholic social doctrine in the Québec unions.

Confessionalism and the staff priest in the syndicate were not to be challenged in the CCCL until the mid-1950s, when it responded to the new trend towards secularization and social democracy.

These stirrings were encouraged by intellectuals within the CCCL or functioning as advisers to it. They included Gérard Pelletier, editor of the CCCL newspaper *Le Travail*, and Pierre Elliot Trudeau, legal adviser to the CCCL on labor relations. The CCCL changed its name in 1960 to the present Confederation of National Trade Unions and dropped its confessionalism and resident priests.

The influence of the church and of moderate reformers like Trudeau and Pelletier was replaced by a new era of militant socialist leaders.[2] Their appearance pushed the syndicates even further ahead on the path to radical change in society than the intellectuals, the new technocracy of the Quiet Revolution or even the emerging separatist parties—the Rassemblement pour l'Indépendance Nationale (RIN) and the Parti Québécois—were yet ready to accept.

In May 1972 Québec's labor movement announced their *Front commun* (Common Front) formed from the three major trade union congresses. Québec stood still more than once in that year as a result of massive strikes in the public sector, and the seizure of company towns as well as radio stations and newspapers by radical union rank and file.

The CNTU issued a manifesto at the time of the formation of the Common Front which boasted of the CNTU's proximity to "the tradition of revolutionary syndicalism." The leaders of the three unions were jailed for defying a court order and for using the occasion to call for revolutionary tactics.

"Breaking the system" was and remains the goal of these three trade-union presidents. They are Louis Laberge, then as now president of the Québec Federation of Labor; Marcel Pepin, who took over the presidency of the CNTU from Jean Marchand in 1963; and Yvon Charbonneau, president of the 70,000-member Québec Teachers' Corporation, which is affiliated with the CNTU.

Mr. Charbonneau's angry outburst five years later during a special management-labor conference called by the Parti Québécois should settle any doubts he has changed his mind about who the enemy is. During this joint seminar, held at the Manoir Richelieu in May 1977, Mr. Charbonneau called the representatives of large companies, such as the presidents of Power Corporation and Steinberg's, "economic terrorists."[3]

The three big labor organizations in Québec together represent almost half a million workers and professionals in government, schools, and industry. In effect, they dominate organized labor. Their eleven-day strike of essential services in April 1972, when hospital workers defied back-to-work injunctions, stopped the province in its tracks.

"In a far more business-like manner than any FLQ cell, Québec's labor leaders. . .made a major effort to set themselves up as a parallel power to the elected government," said *Time* on May 22, 1972.

At the heart of Québec's labor militancy of the 1970s is a growing grass-roots hatred of American capitalism, which is seen by labor leaders as the prime cause for the alienation of Québec society. The complete eradication of capitalism from Québec society is the goal of the far left. With it, they claim, will end the "distortions" of the capitalist state which have caused Québec's high unemployment and assured the dominant role of English-Canadian and foreign business elites.

For Québec's militants—the unions, the *péquistes* restless with Lévesque's moderate policies, and the young unemployed—the final stage of the Québec revolution must be the fully socialist state, not unlike Algeria, Cuba, or Chile under Salvador Allende.

Seen in this light, Jacques Parizeau's pronouncements in favor of economic nationalism, based in part on his strong loathing of the English, are not alarming. But this cultured, British-trained economist, and Premier Lévesque himself, could become the Kerenskys of Québec if separation is not the orderly social transformation they currently propose.

Lévesque has persistently and vociferously resisted all forms of extremism, referring to the nearly catastrophic labor shutdowns of 1972 as the work of "ranting and raving labor leaders."[4]

And while it is true that the PQ victory of 1976, and the percentage of votes for the PQ in the 1970 and 1973 provincial elections, indicate major working-class support, the Parti Québécois under Lévesque has never openly supported such militant labor actions.

"The PQ seems to have succeeded in its purpose;" write the two authors of *The Decolonization of Québec*, "it maintains middle class support by placing itself wholly on the side of law and order. . .while it has held on to the allegiance of the working class by making it even more evident that it was the only party at all sympathetic to its needs and demands."[5]

The ideologies of Québec's militant left have little to do with Canadian political experience. They relate to the Third World and its politics of confrontation.

Québec contains many elements of a Third World country. These include substantial underdevelopment in frontier regions, exploited indigenous peoples, social and economic inequities in the cities from too-rapid urbanization, and the presence of at least two terrorist organizations, including the currently quiescent FLQ (Front de Libération du Québec).

Québec's neo-Marxist writers, some of them long associated with the Parti Québécois, have defined Québec's status within Canada and North America in Third World terms of neocolonialism and dependency on multi-national corporations.

Writing in the journal *Liberté* in 1974, Fernand Ouellette

says, ''I think that one of the dangers of thought and action in Québec is our compliance to helplessness.''

Gérald Godin, poet and ideologue of the non-Marxist left and a Parti Québécois member of the National Assembly, said in a Toronto conference in March 1977 on Québec's future, ''Either you are a nationalist or you are swallowed up by the imperialists.''[6]

''Liberation'' from the dominant U.S. and Anglo-Canadian corporation is understandably seen in Cuban terms and with admiration for the Cuban experience of 1960 of complete nationalization of American branch plants.

The Cuban connection of Québec's terrorists and extreme nationalists has been obscured by the secrecy of their movements and by the public's belief that our relations with Havana have been solely those of a healthy and profitable trade association. But while Canadian financiers and industrialists filled the ranks of the busy Canadian trade missions to Havana during the 1960s, bringing industrial equipment no longer obtainable from the Americans, the ideologues of Fidel Castro were training Québec separatists and terrorists.

In 1968 an informal group of fifteen Québec separatists visited Havana in a propitious year for political tourists: it was *El Año del Guerrillero Heroico* (''The Year of the Heroic Guerrilla''). ''The Québec group. . .signed a declaration of solidarity with the Third World in our struggle for the liberation of Québec,'' wrote Roger Soublière in *Parti Pris*.[7]

During the mid-1960s, when bank robberies (some of them presumably to fill the treasuries of terrorist groups) and bombings turned Montreal into a Montevideo of the north, some of the founders of predecessor movements to the FLQ, such as the ALQ (Armée de la Libération du Québec), were already students in Castro's guerrilla training schools. Here Québec's revolutionaries rubbed shoulders with Algerian, North Vietnamese, Venezuelan, Argentine and Palestinian terrorists. Many of their fellow students had already experienced front-line action against police, army and other reactionary forces in the streets of Algiers, Saigon, Buenos Aires and Amman.

The ALQ and FLQ members in Cuba, who often traveled there as tourists on Canadian passports, might even have been exposed to the elite Boca Chica School for guerrilla training and indoctrination in Havana. During most of the 1960s this school was under the direction of Alberto Bayo, a former general in the Spanish Republican Army defeated during the Spanish Civil War.

What kind of Québec extremists have been trained in Cuba?

George Shoesters, in his late twenties at the time, was a Belgian immigrant and part-time student at l'Université de Montréal. One of the founders of the FLQ in 1962, he was paroled from a Montreal prison in 1967. Shoesters was already in Algeria as far back as 1958, studying revolutionary tactics with the Algerian terrorist organization, the Front de Libération Nationale. He returned to Montreal in time for Fidel Castro's one and only visit to that city in 1959. During 1960-61 Shoesters served as an ''adviser'' to INRA, Castro's huge state-farm development agency, then came back to Canada where he was arrested for extremist acts in Québec.

Another FLQ leader, Gaston Collin, also in his late twenties at the time, was an embittered veteran of the Canadian army, in which he claimed there was massive discrimination against French Canadians. Also paroled from a Montreal prison in the spring of 1968 for terrorist acts, he was in Cuba during 1968-69.[8]

Much of the literature released by the FLQ, such as their mimeo sheet *La Cognée* (''The Axe'') and their later manifestos, including those issued after the kidnapping of British Trade Commissioner James Cross, all had Castro-Cuban ideological overtones. They also bore strong similarity to manifestos released to Uruguayan radio stations and newspapers by the Tupumaros, Uruguay's now-defunct urban guerrilla movement which was operating in strength at the same time as the FLQ.

But the basic ideological inspiration for Québec's terrorist groups came from Cuban socialism and admiration for the philosophy and political action of the martyred guerrilla leader Ernesto "Che" Guevara.

During the October Crisis of 1970, neither the Québec Provincial Police nor the RCMP would admit that there were Cuban-style guerrilla training camps in some of Québec's isolated forest regions, including the ski country of the Laurentians. But press reports at the time claimed the ALQ had a camp at St. Boniface, Québec. And it is a fact that during the FLQ crisis and immediately after, CF-5 squadrons of the Canadian Armed Forces equipped for photographic surveillance made regular sweeps over remote regions of central and northern Québec.

This little-known use of the Canadian Armed Forces is a small portent of wider use of the military in any future development of extremist government in Québec.

While the Canadian military claim they have no plan for any kind of action against Québec, there are several eventualities which should be considered.

The most extreme would be Canadian military penetration of a republic ideologically close to the Communist world, and threatening both post-secessionist Canada and the United States by permitting Soviet or Cuban military bases—a North American Angola in effect.

A more likely prospect would be military intervention within the scope of existing "tasks" assigned to the Canadian military; that is, "aid to the civil power" or protection of internal security. Aid to the civil power in any province can only be used if military assistance is requested by the provincial attorney general.

It is hard to imagine the attorney general in a Parti

Québécois cabinet requesting aid from the federal military. But if he were faced with a major breakdown in the social order due to strikes and lockouts, or a determined effort to unseat an elected separatist government while Québec was still a province, a repeat of the army's role in 1970 would be conceivable.

If Québec achieved independence through violence and not through the peaceful route of constitutional procedure, the federal government might have to use the armed forces in an internal security function.

In the summer of 1977 the Canadian Armed Forces announced the formation of a new Special Service Force. This unit of approximately 3,200 men combines the airborne regiment with selected tank, artillery and helicopter units to form an integrated military element with both "air drop" and ground fighting capability. The Special Service Force was the idea of General Jacques Dextraze, who retired as Chief of the Defence Staff in September 1977.

The stated purpose of the force is to meet our NATO commitment of assistance in the defense of northern Norway against Soviet attack. However, the fact that such a force was established after the election of a strong separatist government in Québec, and is based at Petawawa, the largest army base close to Québec, raises questions about the real purpose of it. Was there another reason why the airborne regiment, Canada's equivalent to the paratroops we see patrolling the streets of other countries during civil disturbances, was moved from its Edmonton base to link up with armored units near Québec?

The military vigorously denied the move was made to bring the unit closer to Québec, even though a primary task of the airborne regiment in Edmonton was to serve as part of Canada's very thin defenses against any Soviet intrusion in our Arctic.

In spite of official denials of preparations to meet a

LOCATION MAP OF THE CANADIAN ARMED FORCES, SHOWI
SUBSTANTIAL BASES AND ACTIVITIES IN QUÉBEC, FEW IN T
NORTH AND ARCTIC.

NATIONAL DEFENCE H.Q. MOBILE BASE
MOBILE COMMAND MARITIME BASE
MARITIME COMMAND TRAINING BASE
MARITIME COMMAND PAC. AIR BASE
TRAINING SYSTEM CAN.DN FORCES STATION
AIR COMMAND MARITIME STATION
COMMUNICATIONS COMMAND AIR STATION
REGIONAL COMMAND H.Q. COMMUNICATIONS STATION
NORTHERN REGION H.Q. AIR SITE

LABRADOR SEA

ON BAY

EASTERN REGION

ATLANTIC REGION

TRAL GION

ATLANTIC OCEAN

Reg.Hewson

Québec crisis, General Dextraze himself was worried enough about the penetration of separatist ideas among the Francophone members of the Canadian Armed Forces to go on speech-making tours of the military bases in Québec. *Le Soleil* of Québec City reported on March 30, 1977 that Dextraze was "making an appeal to the patriotic sense of 'citizens in uniform.' "

During the spring and summer of 1977, two other developments in the Canadian Armed Forces caused speculation that the Department of National Defence was preparing for possible trouble in Québec.

First the department announced a manpower increase of 5,000 (bringing the armed forces to a total of about 85,000) and the purchase of 350 armored vehicle carriers to be built by General Motors of Canada. This is the kind of vehicle used to control street riots or to patrol strategic highways and airports during major civil disorders in many other countries.

Second, the first internal security exercise after the Parti Québécois victory in November 1976 was held not at Petawawa, the usual site for such an activity, but near Meaford, Ontario. It was thought that the Meaford site would draw less public attention, since it is a good distance from the Québec border.

In the outcry against the strong-arm methods used by the Canadian government during the 1970 crisis, a rumor spread that National Guard units in American states bordering on Québec had been secretly authorized to mobilize if Canada were to experience a "Latin-American-style" urban guerrilla upheaval.

U.S. intelligence, it was said, was not deceived by the very small size of the FLQ cells which upset an entire nation; the Brazilian guerrilla leader and author Carlos Marighela, killed in a street ambush in 1969, had emphasized the need for urban guerrillas to form small but intensely activist cells.

His classic text, *Handbook of Urban Guerrillaism*, is used by the provisional Irish Republican Army, Libyan terrorists, and the Palestinian Democratic Front, the most militant arm of the Palestinian Liberation Organization which incidentally had contacts with remnants of the FLQ in the early 1970s.

The rumor of National Guard mobilization instructions was strongly denied, has never been proven, and was probably unfounded. But, given the revelations during 1973-75 of the hemispheric activities of the CIA not only in Latin America but in Canada as well, concern that an extremist government in a Québec republic would provoke U.S. diplomatic or even military action has remained strong.

˛The FLQ terrorists who kidnapped James Cross and killed Pierre Laporte were offered refuge in Castro's Cuba in December 1970 and flown there in a Canadian Armed Forces aircraft. They remained there as "guests" of the Cuban government until they chose the more familiar milieu of France a few years later.

How ironic that their stay in the ideological haven of the Québec terrorist groups should have been totally frustrating and unhappy! In spite of their ideological fraternity with the Cubans, they did not understand the Hispanic milieu. They were clearly not heroes to the Cuban revolutionaries, whose experience in overthrowing a bourgeois society they had hoped to duplicate in Québec, and they were an embarrassment to the Cuban government.

It is frightening to contemplate the future of Québec if union militancy, political extremism and demagogic leadership together are allowed to prevail.

Class warfare has been preached and promulgated by the major trade unions throughout the 1970s.

The Quiet Revolution has been judged a hoax by the working class and many Québec nationalists.

The politicization of teachers' unions and of both professors and student bodies has been a phenomenon of the Québec educational system not experienced anywhere else in Canada.

One of the programs of the Quiet Revolution was a radical reform and expansion of Québec's backward educational system, traditionally dominated by the church. New universities were built and others enlarged, and the province-wide system of secular community colleges called CEGEPs (the French acronym for "colleges of general and professional instruction") were built to create a professional and technical basis for Québec's industrial emergence.

During the late 1960s and early '70s the CEGEPs bred separatist sentiment among students and professors, while the expanded universities gave intellectual content to separatist and socialist thought in Québec. The coming of age of the CEGEP generation helped put the Parti Québécois in power on November 15, 1976.

The 1971 manifesto of the Québec Teachers' Corporation said that "the teacher is a producer of ideology," and that the Québec worker is "colonized by Ottawa and U.S. imperialism."[9]

The teachers' syndicate obviously shared the feeling of the militant writers that the Quiet Revolution was only *rattrapage* when what was needed was *libération*.

The new Republic of Québec may become not the social democracy proposed in the Economic Manifesto, with its mixed use of nationalization and joint ventures, but a form of "people's and workers' state."

The concept of workers' councils, chosen rather than elected, and substituting for trade unions which after all are part of the existing system, has been assessed in many left-wing publications. Workers' councils would go beyond the already controversial principle of executive-labor co-management in industry, to operate in the dominant role they had begun to assume in the brief Marxist experiment in Chile.

A militant and revolutionary Québec republic could become a socialist "Chile of the North" with all its ramifications, including American intervention.

Canada would be next door to a socialist state with intimate ties to the Marxist world.

How soon after independence would the first Algerian, Libyan and Cuban embassies, with their world-wide contacts among terrorist and guerrilla movements, set up shop in Québec City?

When would the first Soviet trade mission arrive? And would its main function be trade, or, as with so many Soviet "trade missions" throughout the Third World, promotion of subversive activities not only in Québec but throughout a smaller and weakened Canada?

Would the Republic of Québec become a Western Hemispheric centre for Communist-bloc activities, more threatening to the security of the United States than Castro's Cuba?

Pentagon scenarios for U.S. military action to control the St. Lawrence Seaway and intimidate a socialist Québec— for example, by using an embargo to destroy Québec's economy as was done with Cuba in 1961—are not in the realm of fantasy. Such scenarios have been the stuff of several National War College student essays, and CIA and U.S. military speculation since the first FLQ bombs exploded in Westmount mailboxes and shopping plazas in 1963.

The dark alternative just outlined would catapult the extremism, terror and anger of the Third World into a North American milieu which has so far viewed its extravagance and violence from afar.

Would not a social democratic Québec republic, seeking the peaceful fulfillment of Lévesque's old plan of *souverain-*

eté association with a post-secessionist Canada, be a more acceptable solution?

NOTES

1. The late President Perón's words resembled those of present Québec labor leaders. Speaking to the CGT early in his first presidency, Perón said: "Under the capitalist regime syndicalism has no option but to fight and fight up to the point of revolution, in order to overthrow the government of capitalism. . . .In order to obtain fair wages, the capitalist regime must be overthrown and a socially just regime set up in its place." *The General Confederation of Labor Listens to Perón*, Office of the President of the Nation (Buenos Aires, 1950).
2. See John D. Harbron, "What Role for the Church in Québec's Changing CNTU?" *Executive*, October 1963, pp. 85-89.
3. Canadian Press report, May 26, 1977.
4. Milner and Milner, *Decolonization of Québec*, p. 211.
5. Ibid, p. 219.
6. Winter conference of the Canadian Institute on Public Affairs, "Canada, the PQ and Us," Toronto, March 5, 1977.
7. *Parti Pris* 5, no. 7 (April 1968).
8. See John D. Harbron, "Québec's guerrillas learned how in Cuba," *Miami Herald*, October 14, 1970.
9. William Johnson, "Three manifestos from organized Québec labor could be the blueprint for class warfare," *Globe and Mail*, December 24, 1971.

5

Concepts of Canadian Sovereignty

5

Part of the heritage of this country. . . .is the purity of
our water, the freshness of our air and the extent of
our living resources. . . . .

For ourselves and the world, we must jealously
guard these benefits. To do so is not chauvinism.

It is an act of sanity in an increasingly irresponsible
world.

Pierre Elliott Trudeau

Canadian efforts to define national goals in the three
decades since World War II have been more diffuse, and
have had much less impact, than Québec's cultural and
political emergence during the same period. Canada is
becoming aware of her huge potential as a nation, but the
intangible pride of nationhood is still hesitant and unsure.

Sovereignty protection and northern development, which
have become acceptable goals in the 1970s, were not
priorities in the immediate postwar era of 1945-1960.
"Sovereignty protection" had overtones of gunboat diplomacy, and suggested that military force might have to be
used to defend our frontiers.

At that time our diplomatic, trade and military thrusts

were being extended overseas towards the North Atlantic community of which we were a vital and founding element.

Canadian sovereignty, if defined at all, might have been articulated in military terms. We prided ourselves on our contribution to the NATO line of defense against the major threat of the 1950s—the increasing military power of Soviet Russia. There were the 500 Canadian-built CF-100 jet interceptor aircraft which filled the NATO and home defense squadrons of the old Royal Canadian Air Force, as well as the destroyer escorts of the Royal Canadian Navy, designed and built in the 1950s to maintain the navy's traditional World War II role of antisubmarine warfare in the North Atlantic.

Canada's military success was matched by her diplomatic prowess as a middle power, not only in NATO but in other international organizations such as the United Nations and the World Bank.

In economic terms, the 1950s offered Canada a comfortable pattern of growth, with plenty of money and public support for a continuing major defense role in Europe. Increasing affluence was assured by our abundance of natural resources, which would always be in demand in the world's industrial nations.

There was little thought, except perhaps by the politicians of the old CCF socialist party, about curbing the indiscriminate sale of nonrenewable resources, and even less about any kind of government control over foreign ownership of our extractive industries.

Nor was much thought given to consolidating our claim to the Arctic. The juridical meaning of "sovereignty" was only beginning to be expressed.

In 1953 Ivan L. Head (who would later become Prime Minister Trudeau's chief adviser on foreign policy), wrote: "Canada's claim to sovereignty in the Arctic has many roots. Discovery, exploration, acquisition by treaty, effective occupation. . .all the ingredients are present."[1]

The effective occupation concept was put in sharper terms in 1958 by Alvin Hamilton, Conservative Minister of Northern Affairs and Natural Resources and one of the Diefenbaker visionaries. "You can hold a territory by right of discovery or by claiming it under some sector theory. But where you have great powers holding different points of view, the only way to hold that territory with all its great potential wealth is by effective occupation."[2]

Canada's claim to the Arctic was justified to a certain extent by the presence of Hudson's Bay Company stores, RCMP posts, religious missions such as those of the Oblate fathers, and various exploration and surveying activities.

However, the American presence in the Arctic during the 1950s was even more conspicious than the Canadian, due to the presence of U.S. military and civilian personnel who built the DEW line radar stations to detect Soviet air attack.

It is true that Arctic development was not entirely ignored by the St. Laurent Liberal governments of the early and mid 1950s, even at the height of our expansionist phase.

St. Laurent was concerned about our claims to the Arctic islands. In 1953 he stated government policy in the House of Commons: "We must leave no doubt about our active occupation and exercise of our sovereignty in these lands right up to the pole."[3]

Renewed commercial interest in the Arctic during St. Laurent's administration led to the formation of the Department of Northern Affairs, with Jean Lesage as its first minister.

But the major changes in our national priorities in the last two decades have come about under the governments of John Diefenbaker and Pierre Elliott Trudeau.

The Diefenbaker Conservatives, who came to power in June 1957, shifted government emphasis away from GNP growth and military expansion towards solution of the growing problems of regional needs and chronic regional economic disparity.

Liberal governments since 1963 have given little credit to the national development policies introduced during the brief Diefenbaker governments.

The Conservative program called "Roads to Resources" supplied about $150 million for railway facilities to make possible the development of mining and related industries at Pine Point on Great Slave Lake. The National Energy Board was also created in 1961, and continues as the chief federal regulatory body for all Canadian energy imports and exports affecting all gas and oil pipeline projects.

Other elements of Conservative national development were renewed interest in the protection of Arctic sovereignty, major efforts to reduce regional disparity in Saskatchewan, Québec and the Maritimes, and the formulation of the National Oil Policy which lasted from 1961 until the 1974 oil crisis. [4]

The Diefenbaker years also succeeded in giving Canada a genuine vision of western and northern development. The former prime minister had trouble transforming the biblical saying that people perish without a vision into strong economic and social policies; nevertheless he aroused in many Canadians what the affluence and materialism of the expansionist 1950s had dissipated.

This was a renewed curiosity about Canada's remaining empty spaces—the kind our ancestors penetrated and conquered—and a desire for a personal rapport with the "unredeemed North." Arctic tourism was given a sudden boost in the Diefenbaker period, mainly by young urban Canadians who wanted to see what Canada was still like "at the end of the line."

The "Arctic Circle" of the early 1960s was more than a geographic term; it was an unusual phenomenon, an informal club of federal public servants in departments serving the North who met regularly in Ottawa homes and offices to share a common enthusiasm about our last frontier.

I am convinced that without the emotionalism of the Diefenbaker vision, in its several impulsive and brief expressions, there could not have been the relatively easy response of Trudeau and his planners to issues of sovereignty protection a decade later. Fifteen years after the Diefenbaker administration, Justice Thomas Berger, chairman of the commission appointed by the Canadian government in 1975 to investigate the impact of gas pipelines on the North, blurted out during a television interview, "It's that part of Canada we all consider to be our emotional heartland."[5]

While Lester Pearson was remembered chiefly as an international diplomat, and lacked the unique Canadian visions of Diefenbaker or Trudeau, he did make some substantial contributions to our hesitant nationalism.

The Canadian flag emerged in 1965 after almost interminable debate, and the Royal Commission on Bilingualism and Biculturalism—the largest, longest and most expensive royal commission in Canadian history—was set up. The B & B Commission was as divisive as the flag debate had been, yet it stirred Canadians into a sort of dialogue on their age-old problems. Its recommendations for a bilingual public service and the use of both official languages in all federal institutions, courts and crown corporations, resulted in Trudeau's Official Languages Act of 1969.

But it was probably Expo '67, a truly dynamic and almost unique outburst of Canadian national identity, and one of the most successful of world fairs, for which the Pearson years will be most remembered.

The Liberal government of Pierre Elliott Trudeau expanded on the Diefenbaker vision of Canadian nationhood. Trudeau decreased Canada's commitment to NATO, while promoting our ties with Latin America and the Third World and concentrating more effectively on hemispheric security and national development.

Within two years of assuming office in April 1968, the new prime minister was the inspiration behind all of the following:

- Foreign Policy Review, May 29, 1968
- Ministerial visit to Latin America, October-November 1968
- Seminar on relations with NATO, Toronto, January 1969
- Seminar on relations with Latin America, Toronto, March 1969
- Defence Policy Review, April 4, 1969
- Arctic Waters Pollution Prevention Bill, passed by Parliament June 9, 1970
- Amendments to the Territorial Sea and Fishing Zone Act of 1964, passed by Parliament June 9, 1970
- White Paper on Foreign Policy, released June 25, 1970

In his superb analysis of Mr. Trudeau's foreign policy, the young scholar Bruce Thordarson says: "Between May 1968 and June 1970 the Canadian Government undertook an extensive reassessment of its foreign and defense policies that for the first time went back to basic principles. Indeed it is unlikely that any government in any country has ever subjected its external relations to such scrutiny."[6]

In his statement of May 29, 1968, Mr. Trudeau revealed the philosophy behind his foreign policy directions: "We wish 'to take a fresh look at the fundamentals of Canadian foreign policy to see whether there are any ways in which we can serve more effectively Canada's current interests, objectives and priorities."[7] He announced that Canada would proceed towards recognition of the People's Republic of China (which took place October 13, 1970), "explore new avenues of increasing our political and economic relations with Latin America. . .where we have substantial interests," and bring about a major reassessment of Canada's military roles.

The Foreign Policy Review led to the ministerial visit to Latin America in the fall of 1968, a four-week blitz of the major countries involving six senior ministers touring in rotation.

The two Toronto foreign-policy study seminars, organized by the Canadian Institute of International Affairs on behalf of the External Affairs Department, placed senior external affairs officials and policy-makers in an uneasy (for them) association with private-sector specialists, academics and journalists. The idea for these seminars was the prime minister's; he envisioned a sort of friendly confrontation, but confrontation nevertheless, to challenge conventional wisdom. The seminars were a part of the prelude to the partial withdrawal from our longstanding NATO military role and the strengthening of our Latin American and Third World commitments.

The Defence Policy Review of April 1969 and the two Arctic sovereignty acts of June 1970 defined in precise terms Trudeau's determination to shift our priorities away from Europe and back to our own hemisphere.

The new priorities of the Canadian Armed Forces were set out in the Defence Policy Review as follows:

(1) The surveillance of our own territory and the protection of our sovereignty;

(2) Defense of North America in cooperation with American forces;

(3) The fulfillment of such NATO commitments as "may be agreed upon";

(4) The performance of such United Nations peacekeeping roles "as we may from time to time assume."

Thus defense of our own territory was given top priority, while our peacekeeping role in NATO and the United Nations was reduced significantly.

At that time, much publicity was devoted to the proposed reduction in our NATO forces from 10,000 to 5,000 and to the cutback in weapons purchases which had cost Canadian taxpayers about $50 billion since 1945. The Canadian military establishment, fed on successive programs of new and increasingly expensive weaponry since the end of World War II, didn't like the review.

These "sharp-end" warriors, whose training and careers were geared to the possibility of a war against Communist powers, resisted the changed priorities. "Now we are supposed to hold hands with Eskimos," mused a frustrated brigadier general in the fall of 1971, in his report to a ministerial task force investigating the management operations of the Department of National Defence during the new restraints period.

The year 1970 saw the passage of the impressive Arctic Waters Pollution Prevention Bill and the Amendment to the Territorial Sea and Fishing Zone Act, both on the same day. The development of the Arctic in the 1970s required measures to protect both sea and land from pollution by accidental leakage from supertanker or drilling rig, and to minimize the negative effects of the new technology of oil and gas transportation on native peoples.

The Arctic Waters Pollution Prevention Bill was designed not only for environmental protection; it was also a sovereignty protection vehicle to be strengthened by the extension of our territorial waters. It gave Canada authority to police within a zone extending 100 miles beyond the Arctic islands.

The boundary was to run equidistant between Greenland and the Arctic islands in the east to a point above Ellesmere Island in the far north and 100 miles west of the Arctic Archipelago in the west, thus enclosing our Arctic waters.

The Arctic Waters Pollution Prevention Bill won unanimous approval in the House of Commons. The third reading on June 9, 1970 made the bill law and paved the way for Trudeau's unprecedented unilateral declaration that Canada would repudiate the jurisdiction of the International Court of Justice in any future international disputes about Arctic pollution.

A sharp protest from the U.S. State Department in

Washington was the predictable result. The official statement read: "The United States regards this unilateral act as totally without foundation in international law and deeply regrets this action." But, as the editorial writers commented when the note was released, the sky did not fall down.

The Amendments to the 1964 Territorial Sea and Fishing Zone Act, passed on the same day as the pollution bill, replaced the country's three-mile territorial limit and nine-mile exclusive fishing zone with a "twelve-mile territorial sea," and provided for the establishment of new fishing zones on both coasts. (On January 1, 1977 the 200-mile territorial zone was established over all of Canada's coastal waters.)

The establishment of "sanitation zones" around our Arctic islands was similar to sovereignty declarations made by Peru, Chile, Ecuador, Argentina and Brazil during the late 1950s and early '60s. In Peru, for example, the breeding practices of the anchovy, whose fish-meal by-product made Peru the world's largest per-capita fish exporter in the early 1970s, could only be protected by the unilateral declaration of an extensive national sea zone.

Professor and political scientist Peyton Lyon of Carleton University applied the apt title "The Trudeau Doctrine" to the two acts assuring Arctic sovereignty and the beginnings of an ecological protection mechanism in the North.

The Trudeau Doctrine was followed throughout the early 1970s in domestic policy measures designed to increase Canada's control over her own economic destiny.

The Foreign Investment Review Act, providing for the establishment of the Foreign Investment Review Agency (FIRA), was passed in 1974.

Petro-Canada, the new state oil corporation, commenced its operations in 1975.

The Canada Development Corporation (CDC) began its activities after Parliament had approved its formation in 1971. This was a decade after a bill calling for such a development corporation was first introduced in Parliament by Walter Gordon, finance minister in the Pearson government.

These agencies were created under the mild stimulus which economic nationalism had in this country during the 1960s. Yet considering that Canada has more direct American investment than all the Latin American republics combined, and that our oil industry is about 70 percent controlled by foreign oil multinationals, control agencies like FIRA and interventionist crown corporations like the CDC or Petro-Canada have very limited powers.

Basically the Liberal Party, which has been in power in this country continuously since the end of World War II with the exception of the six-year Diefenbaker interlude, has not wanted to upset the smooth north-south flow of investment, new plant construction and technological transfer. This flow began in earnest after 1946 when C.D. Howe persuaded American and a few British firms to fill up Canada's empty munitions plants.

The CDC, FIRA and Petro-Canada have so far been fragile and even impotent instruments of national policy. This is in marked contrast to Mexico's regulatory agencies which were described in chapter three.

The Canada Development Corporation does not have the interventionist power of Mexico's NAFINSA.

Petro-Canada has the authority to expand beyond its present frontier oil exploration into refining and maritime oil transport if offshore drilling in the Arctic proves worthwhile. But it by no means dominates the Canadian private oil and gas industry—in fact, the opposite is true.

And FIRA, which in a Mexican context would put the fear of God into foreign firms, has approved many more foreign take-overs or mergers of Canadian companies and more arrivals of new foreign firms than it has rejected.

These three agencies were introduced piece-meal as a response to growing economic nationalism. They were not implemented from any overall policy of state involvement in the private sector based on a brutal relationship with an imperialist power, such as Mexico's experience with the United States.

Walter Gordon's "Buy Back Canada" formula is clearly unworkable in the form he proposed. The Canadian experience is unique in that we have permitted more foreign control of our economy than any other advanced industrial state in history. To buy back the thousands of American firms operating in this country, or even a portion of them, is simply beyond Canada's means.

Yet nations much poorer than Canada have embarked successfully on intensive programs of economic nationalism. They do not try to "buy back" foreign-controlled plants; they work out joint ventures with the state or local private capital as major participants, or licensing and technology-sharing arrangements, as we have seen in Mexico. They are able to do this under the impetus of intense nationalistic ideologies such as we have not yet experienced in Canada.

Canadians have remained divided on the advantages or hazards of foreign control over their economy, partly because along with heavy foreign investment has come one of the world's highest standards of living.

The "will" which Prime Minister Trudeau often speaks about for finding Canadian solutions to Canadian problems has not yet been applied to the problem of restricting foreign control. Canada must still find an answer to this most vital area of national economic policy-making.

NOTES

1. Ivan L. Head, "Canadian Claims to Territorial Sovereignty in the Arctic, *McGill Law Journal*, no. 3, 1963, p. 210.
2. Ibid, p. 213.
3. Ibid.
4. The National Oil Policy operated on the simple principle of

buy cheap and sell dear. Québec and the Maritimes imported what was then cheap crude from Venezuela and the Middle East. Ontario and Western Canada used oil from Alberta. The policy required that at least 600,000 barrels per day be exported to the United States, where oil was more expensive than in Canada.

5. Television documentary on the Mackenzie Valley gas pipeline, OECA Television, Toronto, June 16, 1976.

6. Bruce Thordarson, *Trudeau and Foreign Policy: A Study in Decision-Making* (Toronto: Oxford University Press, 1972), p. 2.

7. ''Canada and the World: A Policy Statement by Prime Minister Pierre Elliott Trudeau,'' *Statements and Speeches*, Department of External Affairs, Ottawa, no. 68/17 (May 29, 1968), p. 7.

6

Canada Without Québec

6

Those who loved the older traditions of Canada may
be allowed to lament what has been lost, even though
they do not know whether or not that loss will lead to
some greater political good.

But lamentation falls easily into the vice of
self-pity. To live with courage is a virtue, whatever
one may think of the dominant assumptions of one's
age.

George Grant, *Lament for a Nation*

Québec will enter independence with both a strong sense
of national purpose and a will to survive.

A Canadian national identity will not be quite so easy to
achieve, even though the obstacle of Québec's French
cultural attachment will be removed.

Still, I do not believe that the union forged in 1867 can be
shattered even by the loss of a sixth of its territory and over
a quarter of its population. Though severely shaken by such
an experience, the Canadian Confederation will not
disintegrate into a succession of separate communities as
the Austro-Hungarian Empire did after the military collapse
of 1918.

Canada without Québec should not turn inward upon herself, bitter, resentful about the new republic, a hemispheric Rhodesia in which Canadian institutions sorely bruised by the secession refuse to rise to new challenges.

What the Canadian nation must do now is to shape strategies to cope with all the problems that will arise when Québec separates.

Perhaps the most obvious problem will be the economic pull from the United States. Below the surface of American public life still lies the belief in "Manifest Destiny." It is instilled in successive generations of American school children through history books which portray the Americans as having conclusively won the War of 1812, and which play down the imperialist feat-of-arms called the Mexican War.

The Jeffersonian coup of buying the vast Louisiana heartland from a cash-shy Napoleon on the verge of conquering a European empire, deprived the French forever of political power in the Western Hemisphere. Jeffersonian expansionism still lives, in an America ever in need of new resources, ready to be resurrected against a Canada in disarray. The American experiments in ruling Alaska, Hawaii, Puerto Rico and the Virgin Islands, all originally colonial outreaches of the expanding republic, could easily be adapted to parts of Canada truly weary of the struggle for national identity.

In the months following the Parti Québécois victory of November 1976, the American press was filled with letters from readers who were unclear about the Canadian dilemma but perfectly aware of the ease with which the remnants of our country could fall into the lap of Uncle Sam.

The most articulate of these, almost a model for the future, appeared in the *New York Times*, with a map showing Québec as a blackened portion of a large white Canadian maple leaf. Correspondent Dennis E. Kelly wrote:

> With their resources the western provinces would drive a very hard bargain for the benefit of their association with the U.S. That joinder would be historic, a Jeffersonian coup for a U.S. president.
>
> Given today's uncertainty, a present interest in a future state or perhaps commonwealth offers very interesting possibilities to U.S. investors; in fact an investor of size might encourage and even invest in a Québec moving toward independence in order to advance his interests in the West.

Kelly then mentioned the alternative which I believe will emerge if we start to develop strategies for the possibility of Québec's separation:

> Unknown, of course, is Canada's reaction. If separation is perceived as advancing U.S. interests, Canadian nationalism might very well emerge and bring home the common interests of the squabbling provinces.[1]

If separation occurs, the political fabric that we wrought in 1867 will be badly damaged. Ottawa will be a forlorn city, stripped of its credibility as the federal capital, separated by only a river from the enthusiastic new republic on the other shore.

The economic fabric, which has already deteriorated in recent years, will also be sorely hit.

Former Finance Minister John Turner spoke out frankly on Canada's poor political and economic performance during a Toronto speech in 1976: "Not only is Canada at the bottom line for credit among other countries, but we are now on the list of countries of political risk."[2]

The severe devaluation of the Canadian dollar in the summer of 1977 to 92 cents U.S. was a warning of the loss of confidence by the world's money markets in Canada's economic and political performance.

In early August 1977, the *Wall Street Journal*

editorialized on the decline in Canada's ability to perform competitively and the failure of the Trudeau government to control either inflation or chronically high unemployment.

During 1977 some New York financiers even suggested the Canadian dollar should be allowed to drop as low as 85 cents. What kept it from dropping that low after the election of the separatist government in Québec was the continued goodwill which even the hard-nosed financial community was still prepared to extend on behalf of Canada.

The advantages of a devalued dollar for Canadian exports, especially newsprint, which is sold to the U.S. in American dollars, were offset by the growing cost of imports and capital coming into Canada. This means higher costs to Canadians, both for the products we buy and to manufacture the goods we export.

Canada's industrial strength will also be threatened by Québec's departure. Such major national export-oriented industries as pulp and paper and minerals will be virtually cut in two.

Will the remaining industries be granted subsidies to help them survive? Will they be given tax relief, which is needed especially in the Canadian mining industry presently crippled by duplicate federal and provincial taxes?

If the economic common market between Canada and Québec is rejected by the politicians, will crippling tariff walls be raised between the two new countries? What will happen to our already narrow competitive margin on the world market?

Will the powerful multinationals which had already dominated most Canadian industries before separation wish to take an even stronger controlling position in a politically weak, post-secessionist Canada?

Canadian government impotence in the face of multinational corporations was clearly revealed once again during the summer of 1977 in the oil industry. Energy Minister Alastair Gillespie admitted he could not control what the oil companies would do with new funds coming to them from domestic oil price increases which were intended to finance further Canadian energy development.

The best he could guarantee, in an industry that is 70 percent foreign-owned, was that the cash flows of oil companies here would be monitored to make sure that extra profits were not being siphoned off in payments to shareholders or for oil exploration outside Canada.[3]

It is hardly surprising that the Canadian Manufacturers' Association has tended to propose rather lukewarm policies for local ownership of branch plant expansion in Canada when the CMA president was so often a senior executive of a large U.S. branch plant!

An industrial strategy for Canada has been on the minds of cabinet ministers, senior bureaucrats and the various trade associations during most of the 1960s and '70s. Such a strategy will be essential to preserve the Canadian industrial presence on world markets when Québec will be just one more competitor.

We should start investigating at once the ways in which small nations like Holland, Belgium and Switzerland have been innovative and competitive with an industrial base much smaller than our own.

We should also study the Japanese strategy, in which private industry, the banking system and government have worked together under "administrative guidance" to form the foreign trade policy which has made Japan one of the world's leading postwar trading nations.

Canadian institutions in the public sector have tended to reject strategic thinking, largely because our basically conservative society has been more successful with social experiments which were carried out voluntarily. These have included the multicultural experiment, the peaceable and well-managed urban communities which have avoided the horrendous mistakes of American cities, and the model of an officially bilingual state. Also, the very word "strategy" conjures up images of the German general staff, the Pentagon, a Latin American war college, or even the secret plans of the Canadian Armed Forces.

Nor should we blame only our industrialists for failing to propose or implement long-range plans. Our politicians, diplomats and public servants involved in the decision-making process are also to blame.

A geopolitical view of a Canadian future without Québec is unpopular, not only because it assumes Québec will leave, but because the country is dominated at present by antigrowth attitudes.

Nevertheless, it is clear that some kind of interventionist strategy will be essential if we want to save Canadian nationhood after Québec goes.

A very senior public servant, one of the important decision-makers in his Ottawa ministry, said to me: "We need a strategy which will save the south, populate the north. To save Confederation we need a goal to transcend the federal-provincial restrictions and *cul de sacs*—an unorthodox model."

Part and parcel of an industrial strategy for Canada will be a deterministic plan for development and growth in the North and Arctic. This neglected part of Canada will be the territorial counterweight to the loss of Québec, and will help to restore confidence in Canada's strength.

Futuristic models for growth, settlement and industrial relocation, controversial as they seem to us, are being used by the Brazilians in their huge Amazon territory, and by the Venezuelans in their Guyana industrial complex.

The Arctic has long been part of the Canadian subconscious. The French historian and geographer André Siegfried felt its power on Canadian nationhood twenty years ago: "The North is always there like a presence. It is the background of the picture without which Canada could not be Canada."[4] A comprehensive plan for the Arctic could give Canadians a broader understanding of their hemispheric identity, and yet it has rarely been a major element in public policy.

Our neglect of the North has produced unfortunate consequences. Rumblings for a more separate identity and even for self-government are already emerging from the native populations of our Yukon and North West Territories—"colonies", if you like, of Ottawa. They represent frustrations that have been heard before in our history, for example when Upper and Lower Canada chafed against an imperial system that stifled social and political aspirations.

The Dene and the Inuit, who inhabit the entire land space of the NorthWest Territories and the Arctic islands, propose the formation of autonomous communities within Canadian federalism, politically self-governing and economically reliant on traditional forms of cooperativism in food gathering and craft industries.

The total population of Dene and Inuit is about 40,000 once entirely nomadic people who have been more or less forced into dependency on the white world for their livelihood.

Their claims to the Arctic are based on prior rights of land settlement, and the Dene nation, in particular, insist that treaties signed with the government at the end of the nineteenth century and the beginning of the twentieth involved fraud and coercion and should be terminated.

The region claimed by the Inuit, which they call *Nunavut* ("Our Land"), covers all the Arctic islands, including the giant Baffin Island, and about three-quarters of the present North West Territories. The Dene nation claims the rest of the North West Territories: the lands surrounding Great Slave and Great Bear Lakes and extending west to the borders of the Yukon Territory and south to the northern boundaries of British Columbia, Saskatchewan, Alberta and Manitoba.

The failure of all federal governments so far to settle

these massive and all-embracing land claims before decisions are made about the importation of more technology into the North is the basis of the native peoples' dissatisfaction.

The Dene and Inuit claims for self-government within Canada could be dangerous. It is conceivable that the Canadian government would deal with these claims in much the same way that the racist Republic of South Africa has dealt with its natives. The white South African government has begun a program of placing large black racial communities in separate nations.

The first of these so-called independent states is the Republic of the Transkei, announced by Pretoria in the fall of 1976 but so far recognized by no other country in the world except South Africa itself. It appears to be simply a ploy by the white South African government to rid itself of large black majorities.

The indigenous peoples of the Canadian North, who have already been victims of many kinds of racial prejudice and exploitation, could conceivably experience even more of this if their determined claims for political independence within Canadian territory are ever accepted by the federal government. However, Prime Minister Trudeau has stated that he would never agree to the establishment of communities in the North on the basis of race alone.

A more predictable dispute involving our northern territory would be Québec's claim to the 116,000 square miles of Labrador assigned in 1927 by the British Privy Council to the crown colony of Newfoundland.

A future Republic of Québec would consider invalid the decision of 1927 because it was made by an "imperialist power."

The present geographical size of Québec was determined through extensions of her original territory by the federal government in 1898 and 1912 to include the District of Ungava, also known as "New Québec." The District of

Ungava had been part of the vast North West Territory purchased from the Hudson's Bay Company in 1869 by the government of Sir John A. Macdonald.

The Labrador boundary remained undefined until 1927. But its coastal regions were explored and penetrated by aggressive missionaries, such as the Grenfell Mission, and by fishermen and settlers from the self-governing British crown colony of Newfoundland.

It was to this crown colony, which did not become a province of Canada until 1949, that the huge territory cutting deep into the present Québec was awarded by England, rousing much nationalist opposition in Québec.

The dispute became sharper when the period of exploitation of Labrador's iron ore and hydro-electric power resources began in the early 1960s.

Although Labrador did not belong to Québec in the first place, a revolutionary regime could nevertheless follow the example of Panama, which has demanded the "return" of the Panama Canal which it never owned and did not build. A campaign for *Québec irridenta* ("Québec unredeemed") would demand that the territory of the new nation reach to its "legitimate final extension."

If Newfoundland remains within Confederation, Canada and Québec could eventually find themselves in serious conflict over this rich territory.

If Canada is going to define long-range plans to serve her domestic needs, she will have an excellent model in Brazil—another huge western nation which, like Canada, is searching for new directions, although admittedly under the unsavory rule of its army and conservative technocrats. The recent spectacular growth of Brazil as an export nation demonstrates the effectiveness of a strong economic strategy.

Brazil and Canada are remarkably similar in their need to relate the development of huge hinterlands (Arctic and

Amazon) to domestic growth and foreign policy directions.

In 1972, Brazilian planning minister João Paulo dos Reis Velloso outlined what he called "New Dimensions for Brazilian Society: National Integration, Social Integration and External Strategy." Identifying Brazil, India and Canada as "intermediate or candidate powers" (candidates for a larger future world role), he defined Brazilian international policy in terms of domestic needs.

Brazilian foreign relations, said Velloso, were to be conducted "in consonance with the national development strategy, orienting them to the objectives of the most rapid possible growth, modernization and greater competitive power of the national economy."[5]

The Brazilian strategy has resulted in annual growth double that of Canada's (until inflation took its toll in 1975); and to a definition of lead industries which would spearhead Brazil's industrial development and export programs.

Many Brazilian industries, which in the late 1940s were at about the same low level of output as similar Canadian ones, have surged into an export phase which has seen Brazilian shoes, textiles and car parts penetrating the Canadian and other new overseas markets for the first time.

The Brazilian pulp and paper industry, declared a lead industry under the plan, has also expanded into world export markets. Brazilian tree farms, utilizing the eucalyptus tree, which reaches maturity in seven years compared to about fifteen for Canadian pine, are undergoing expansion financed by Spanish, West German and American capital. By 1980, it is estimated, our own pulp and paper industry will face competition from Brazilian newsprint and pulp inside the Canadian domestic market.

Brazilian exports to Canada, already diversified enough to have generated a growing Brazil-Canada trade pattern, are shipped here in Brazilian ships built under an incentive program which has made possible a domestic shipbuilding industry.

Since Brazil, like Canada, must estimate high shipping charges from imports in foreign bottoms as a deficit in the balance of payments, the Brazilian government authorized a tax on all imports in non-Brazilian ships. That sum is maintained in a ship stabilization fund from which the shipyards can borrow to build new facilities. The program has blossomed. Dutch and Japanese shipbuilding subsidiaries, as well as domestic shipyards, have built what is now the second largest merchant fleet in the Western Hemisphere after the American. Brazilian designed and built cargo ships, strengthened for operations in ice, ply our seaway each season. Incredibly, there are no such deep-sea cargo ships built in Canada and operating under the Canadian flag on the seaway and Great Lakes system.

It probably helps to have generals and single-minded technocrats in charge of government to get this kind of plan moving. Yet the Brazilian shipbuilding formula has no particular ideology. It is a simple carrot-and-stick philosophy of taxing foreign carriers at one end to supply funds for state subsidies to the national shipbuilding industry at the other.

Canada's failure in the decades since World War II to formulate comprehensive plans for our shipping needs has been unforgivable. Piecemeal policies and short-term federal assistance schemes for the shipyards are the best the federal government has been able to come up with. It is now too late, given the high cost of labor, for Canada to build a competitive national merchant marine using the Brazilian formula.

It is possible that the new Québec nation will apply a Brazilian-type formula, because nationalism may outweigh the high cost of building a state shipping fleet from scratch. Also, Québec already has Canada's largest and most versatile shipyards: Marine Industries Limited at Sorel and Canadian Vickers Limited and Canada Steamship Lines at Montreal.

Two American academic specialists on Brazilian planning techniques have suggested that the creation and consistent implementation of such techniques have given Brazil "a destiny" and a "potent combination of pragmatic power strategies and ideological fervor."[6] I am afraid the same cannot be said for Canada.

The difference, of course, is that where Mr. Trudeau and his less-deterministic technocrats have been more concerned with "values" in Canadian society, the tougher-minded Brazilians have a freer hand to manipulate the system into new "directions." As Brazilian businessmen and government officials keep repeating on their trade missions, "For us, the time for rhetoric is over." Quite an admission for Latin Americans!

Our loathing of geopolitical solutions aside, a Canadian version of the Brazilian development strategy will be essential as we face the crisis of separation.

In Canadian history of the 1960s and '70s, I can detect only two government efforts at long-term strategies of the kind we need for an uncertain Canadian future.

The first was the Trudeau Doctrine and Foreign Policy Review of 1970. Mr. Trudeau's newly appointed advisers, many of them from industry, were filled with fresh ideas for a stronger Canadian sovereignty, and the Trudeau years began brilliantly with a major emphasis on long-range planning and strategies for the future.

The Trudeau Doctrine, if it had been followed through with the formulation of specific social and economic planning policies, would have supplied the guideline we now need in the development of the North. It tried to concentrate at one and the same time on our needs for economic growth and the advancement of the quality of life and the harmonious environment, but went no further.

The Trudeau Doctrine and Foreign Policy Review priorities seem to have disappeared like an Arctic morning mist, subverted by the pressure of other events, victims of the inertia in the big, cynical government bureaucracies.

The other attempt at strategy formation was the Mid-Canada Development concept of the imaginative, multi-faceted Richard Rohmer. This was a proposal for industrial growth and substantial human settlement in the "Mid-Canada" region between our populous south and our Arctic; "the great green boreal forest which stretches through the mid-north from coast to coast."[7]

The Mid-Canada Development Conference of 1969-70, sponsored by government and private industry, used the talents of perhaps 150 experts from all phases of industrial, academic and governmental activity affecting the region. Identifying itself as "the first attempt to think out ways in which Canadian urban society and Canadian economic life should be oriented towards Canada's geographic location,"[8] it produced important working papers in all major areas of industrial, ecological, cultural and corporate activity.

However, the Rohmer Mid-Canada Development scheme, like the Trudeau Doctrine, seems to have been delivered to the most inaccessible bottom drawer in Ottawa.

Have any strategies emerged from the Canadian private sector during the 1970s, if not from the government in Ottawa?

By turning to western Canada, with its large private resource industries, we are clearly closer to the kind of industrial strategies less frequently developed by eastern Canadians.

Several private corporations, which must consider their long-term needs and goals, have linked resources exploitation and transportation technology into systems designed more for the 1980s and '90s than for the present decade. This kind of integrated planning is being used by Dome Petroleum Limited of Calgary, a Canadian company.

Dome Petroleum has been brought to national prominence by the much-publicized hazards involved in its $300-million program to drill for oil in the Beaufort Sea. The Beaufort drillings represent the latest stage in the company's activities in Arctic oil and gas extraction, which began in 1958.

The global oil crisis since late 1973 has stimulated new interest in previously ignored offshore oil fields and has created more respect for Dome's long-term strategies in the minds of skeptics and conservative public servants.

In June 1977 Gordon Harrison, president of Canadian Marine Drilling Limited, Dome's drilling subsidiary, said that the Beaufort Sea operations "could become an oil and natural gas field as important as the huge Prudhoe Bay field off the North Slope of Alaska," and that production from this facility alone could "supply Canada's needs in oil for the next sixteen years."[9]

In April and May of 1977, Jack Gallagher, the chairman and chief executive officer of Dome Petroleum, a quiet but very persuasive oilman and futurist, concluded a series of proposals to federal cabinet ministers for an Arctic marine transportation system for the 1980s.

The system will be based on a giant 150,000-horsepower icebreaker driven by conventional (non-nuclear) propulsion, which will make it possible for ships to move through heavy Arctic ice from the Beaufort Sea to east coast Canadian and American ports.

Dome's immense icebreaker will have twice the power of the world's largest conventional icebreaker, now in use by the Soviet Union. It will serve as a "marine locomotive," as Gallagher puts it, guiding large icebreaker tankers filled with liquefied natural gas, as well as ice-reinforced supply and drill ships.

To design this ship Mr. Gallagher hired the chief naval architect of Finland's Wärtsilä O.Y. & A.B. shipyard, the world's leading icebreaker builder. Wärtsilä has already designed and built several of the largest conventionally powered icebreakers being used by the USSR on the Baltic Sea and along the Soviet northern sea route.

Dome's icebreaker has the support of the Canadian government. It will be built in an eastern Canadian shipyard at a cost of about $125 million, and will enter regular Arctic-east coast service by 1980. The federal government was contemplating building a smaller, nuclear-propelled icebreaker which would cost an estimated $350 million. Thus Dome will have taken the federal government off the hook, as one company official describes it, by building an icebreaker geared to a commercial purpose for less than half what it would cost the government. [10]

This long process of very costly exploration and development, from which Dome Petroleum will derive no profit until years hence when an Arctic transport facility is completed, represents strategic long-range planning of the kind the government has rarely initiated.

It is true that the federal government has encouraged corporate planning by instituting a 200-percent tax write-off program for Canadian oil and gas companies engaged in multi-million-dollar resources projects, so long as they are wildcat wells which represent an outlay in excess of $5 million each. This has permitted Dome to generate $35 million from corporate sources to meet its other commitments as an integrated oil and gas company serving western Canada and the United States.

But the fact remains that government planning for Arctic development of the kind initiated by this impressive Canadian company seems impossible at present given the multi-faceted structure of government in this country.   To illustrate: in the late 1960s the Department of Transport prepared a study of government shipping fleets which was never made public. The study revealed that there were seven different and often overlapping operators of Canadian government shipping services. These included the navy, under the Department of National Defence; the Department of Transport, which operates our existing icebreakers and has the largest government shipping fleet in Canada; the former National Harbours Board; the Canadian Coast Guard; the Royal Canadian Mounted Police; and two government ministries, Environment and Fisheries.

In the same way, the many layers of government— federal, territorial and municipal—which have a direct or indirect role in the Arctic, or more precisely in the Yukon and North West Territories, are too enmeshed in bureaucratic method to generate any single long-term and workable policy for that region's growth and development. The federal departments of Northern Affairs, Transport, Environment, Fisheries, National Defence, Health and Welfare, and Justice all have a finger in the pie of Arctic administration.

The regional governments of the Yukon and the North West Territories cannot act independently of the federal government; nor can the more informal administrations which exist among the Inuit and Indian communities.

All this bureaucracy and conflicting government activity is directed at one-third of our national territory where the total population does not exceed 100,000 people.

What the Canadian North will need as it assumes greater importance in a nation without Québec, is a single overall administration not unlike the Soviet Union's GLAVSEV-MORPUT, the Main Administration of the Northern Sea Route.

GLAVSEVMORPUT has authority to develop industry, invest in town-site expansion, operate shipping services and icebreaker functions along the entire northern Arctic coast of the USSR, engage in extensive ice, under-ice and oceanographic research, and advise the Soviet Navy on safety measures for its Arctic warship movements. Soviet ice forecasting methods as developed by this huge state agency have set a pattern for scientific activities in this field by other Arctic nations.

GLAVSEVMORPUT has existed within the Soviet state apparatus since 1933, and suffers from the constant bureaucratic snarls of the Russian state system. Fortunately, such an agency in Canada could be protected against excessive bureaucratization by the watchdog roles of a critical Parliament and an equally critical private sector.

The federal government's failure to make comprehensive plans for Canada's development is due to other factors besides the complexity of overlapping departmental jurisdictions. Professors Donald H. Thain and Mark C. Baetz of the University of Western Ontario School of Business Administration have written:

> Although there are many reasons why Canada lacks satisfactory strategic planning, one of the most important is the problem of government organization.
>
> While it is relatively bureaucratic, out-of-date, inflexible, resistant to change and low in motivation, perhaps its greatest single weakness is that there is no provision for broad integration of national planning and action short of the cabinet.
>
> . . .In spite of the political and organizational resistance. . .an effective strategic planning centre is the greatest immediate need of the Canadian government organization.[11]

Professors Thain and Baetz have also linked the federal government's failure at strategic planning to its failure to solve the growing problems in federal-provincial relationships. One of these problems is the need for decentralization.

It is already clear that the token relocation of a few Crown corporations to western Canada—the National Mint in Winnipeg, Petro-Canada in Calgary and the head office of the Canada Development Corporation in Vancouver—hasn't worked.

Decentralization means many things and is admittedly complex. But in its simplest form it means granting the provinces greater authority over taxation, the pricing, marketing and export of their natural resources, and regional development.

At present, federal and provincial departments of health, regional development, transport and finance compete with each other over jurisdiction and tax sharing. These conflicts, and debate over formulas for revenue-sharing, have been the stuff of many federal-provincial conferences, which a frustrated René Levésque has called "the Chinese water-torture treatment."

Decentralization after Québec has left will be imperative because the provinces will demand concessions from a weak central government as the price of keeping the rest of the Canadian Confederation intact.

Indeed, decentralization of many powers of the federal government to the provinces, and an industrial strategy for Canada without Québec, are the two main challenges in long-range planning facing the country.

The obvious question which must be answered first is: would economic development in a post-Québec Canada permit continued domination by outside investment and the foreign-owned enterprise? Or do we want tighter control over the activities of outside interests in our economy?

When we've decided once and for all how much foreign control we want, decentralization of government and an industrial strategy will be developed in tandem.

The provinces would have to accept that it would be the role of the federal government to formulate a strong industrial strategy. In return, the federal government would turn over to the provinces greater authority in regional development.

New formulas for cooperation between multi-national corporations and nationalistic governments have emerged throughout the world since Walter Gordon espoused his unworkable "Buy Back Canada" formula in the early 1960s.

The August 1977 issue of *Fortune* magazine contains an important assessment of the ways in which multi-national corporations have recently begun functioning in overseas markets as minority partners and developers of technology sharing, more and more often receiving a percentage of earnings or royalties rather than functioning through a branch plant.

It cites the case of the two multinational oil giants, Exxon and Shell, which dominated the Venezuelan oil industry before it was nationalized in January 1976. *Fortune* claims they are doing better in their new relationship with PetroVen, the state oil corporation which succeeded them, than they did as owners of the Venezuelan oil industry. This is due to the substantial fees paid by PetroVen to the foreign oil firms for their assistance in managing the state-run corporation, as well as competitive prices for Venezuelan crude shipped to their American refineries.

The same report emphasizes that such deals have been negotiated (or are at least possible) in almost every country except Canada. "Ironically, Canada, which among advanced nations is perhaps the most rabidly opposed to American investment, may have the most to lose from discouraging this investment."[12]

These innovative arrangements between the public and private sectors, which we have already examined in the case of Mexico, must become part of the Canadian economic picture. For example, there could be "trade-offs" between the foreign-owned oil industry in this country and an expanding Petro-Canada, our own state oil agency.

A future federal public service could perhaps be revitalized by "borrowing" executives from private industry during a time of severe national crisis.

This method was applied with much success during World War II by C.D. Howe, then minister of munitions and supply, who brought capable corporate executives into the government for the war's duration. They were paid a token dollar a year by the government for their services, while continuing to receive regular salaries from their own companies.

Many of the temporary wartime crown corporations established during the period between 1940 and 1946 began their operations under management borrowed from industry. These "C.D. Howe men" were later instrumental in directing Canada's postwar boom, because their wartime experience in Ottawa had given them an understanding of the government-industry relationship.

For now, though, decisions in all the vital areas of our economy—decentralization, an industrial strategy, a policy on foreign ownership—are ones which the federal government appears incapable of initiating. It remains convinced that the inevitable—the need to plan a national economy without Québec—will never happen.

At the federal level there is no parallel to the strategic planning of the Parti Québécois. With all its imperfections, the Economic Manifesto represents the only strategic planning currently being proposed by any government in this country.

As I suggested earlier in this chapter, Ottawa after Québec's departure will be a depleted city. Its formulas for holding the country together will have failed. Its bureaucracy will be discredited. Its ranks will be reduced by the departure of many of its Francophone members to work for the new Québec state. Canada will need a new capital, a symbol of the new directions we will take after Québec's departure.

A dynamic western Canada, which has chafed under the pre-secessionist division of power in favor of the east (Ontario and Québec), will demand parity in the post-Québec Canadian nation. I visualize Alberta and not

Ontario as the new seat of the federal government.

I propose that Edmonton be considered for the new federal capital. Edmonton is a Brasilia of the north, a city symbolically located between the southern industrial sector and the Arctic frontier. It is already the jumping-off point for the Arctic, and would be the logical site for the new Canadian equivalent to the Soviet GLAVSEVMORPUT, if such an agency should be established. It was originally laid out as a large frontier community, and already has the administrative machinery of a provincial capital.

Edmonton is also close to Calgary, which is the heart of Alberta and an important centre for resource-based industries such as oil, gas, petrochemicals and food-processing. Calgary and Edmonton already display the kind of cooperation between industry and government which has fallen apart in eastern Canada. As a result Alberta under Premier Peter Lougheed is becoming an industrialized province, a "Ruhr of the West."

My belief is that a federal bureaucracy centered in Edmonton, next door to the dynamic business and investment climate of Calgary, would be forced to cast off the caution, conventional wisdom and laziness which have permeated the public service in Ottawa. The kinds of new relationships between multinationals and governments which are already emerging in other countries around the world could be more quickly developed in the West than in the present atmosphere of Ottawa.

The most clearly identifiable problem in maintaining a single geography after separation is the future of the Atlantic provinces, presumably cut off from Canada by the new Republic of Québec. A Canadian government centered in the West would isolate the Maritime region even further. A problem unresolved since Confederation—the promise to integrate the Atlantic provinces economically with the rest of Canada—will still remain.

The gloomy prospect of Maritime isolation has been more

honestly exposed in the media than the place of the West in a Canada without Québec.

Nova Scotian writer Harry Bruce, in an article called "Atlantic Orphans," outlined what he called "a sad confusion of predictions" of the "unthinkable."[13]

There is the prospect of union with New England, easier said than done for Newfoundland, which is more remote from that part of the United States than New Brunswick, Prince Edward Island or Nova Scotia.

There is the option of a merger of the four Atlantic provinces into a separate Maritime nation. They would then be even more vulnerable to bad world economic conditions than they are at present, because they would no longer have federal subsidization. For Newfoundland, such a solution would mean a return to her pre-Confederation status, which during the Depression years of the 1930s saw her wholly dependent on the British motherland.

The third option is an association with Canada not unlike that of East Pakistan with West Pakistan before the eastern sector became Bangladesh in 1971. Hopefully a land corridor between the two Canadas could be negotiated with Québec.

In spite of all the unfulfilled promises of Confederation, and the geographic awkwardness, this third option might be best for the Maritimes. Not only is it a part of Canada where the traditions of the British monarchy have remained strong, but it is the region which rejected American republicanism when the United Empire Loyalist exiles came to New Brunswick and Nova Scotia from the former thirteen colonies in the early 1780s.

The future of the Maritimes is not as gloomy as Mr. Bruce suggests. One of the largest work forces in the region will continue to be in the operations of Maritime Command based in Halifax, with its related support and supply activities throughout the economy. Canada will want to preserve her three-ocean status and to continue her traditional role as an antisubmarine warfare participant in NATO. A further role of Canada's Atlantic bases will be surveillance of the new 200-mile territorial waters limit; and the east coast fisheries will remain important to the Canadian economy.

Related to all the above activities will be the Maritime shipbuilding industry, often underutilized in the past because of having to share government contracts with Québec's shipyards for political reasons. The long-term subsidization program denied the shipbuilding industry before Québec's departure will probably have to be extended to both west and east coast shipyards.

A post-Québec federal government could establish a separate Ministry of Atlantic Affairs to give the region a permanent place in federal cabinets. Such a ministry would work closely with the federal fisheries, defense and environment departments, and the Department of Regional Economic Expansion which would then concentrate on the economic development needs of the Atlantic provinces.

I have said earlier that the monarchical tradition weakened Canada's hemispheric identity by emphasizing her ties with Europe. Yet need this always be the case?

Québec, the province which resisted monarchy the most, will be gone. Many Canadians who were opposed to our monarchical ties in the past, or at best lukewarm towards them, would now see the value of maintaining that important distinction between Canada and the United States.

The British monarchy was never more a Canadian monarchy than during the astutely planned visits of the royal family to our Arctic during the 1970s. The Queen's Arctic visit in June 1970 did more to legalize Canadian claims to the Arctic, when these were being challenged officially by the United States, than any efforts on Canada's part. This use of the royal presence to legitimize our Arctic claims might not have been needed if the Trudeau Doctrine had offered a scheme for the development of the Arctic.

Canada will be a lonely nation after Québec's departure, needing more than ever to be a part of the cohesiveness of something stretching around the world, like the British Commonwealth.

And even if Canada were to become a republic, it would in no way affect our membership in the Commonwealth. Most of the member nations at the present time are republics, rather than monarchies owing allegience to the British Crown. They include India, Nigeria, Tanzania, Kenya, Guyana, and Sri Lanka. Jamaica, which has beome an important spokesman for Third World issues in Commonwealth meetings, was in the process of a national referendum on republican status as this book was being written. Yet the Commonwealth shows no signs of weakening or breaking up in spite of its overwhelmingly republican membership.

Continued royal visits and active membership in the British Commonwealth could, I believe, strengthen the Canadian national identity without in any way hindering our hemispheric identity, until truly indigenous values for a post-Québec state are worked out.

The gloomy prognoses that Québec on her own can only stumble, and that what is left of Canada can only disintegrate, are not in my view justified.

If the historical determinism propounded by Professor Bolton is to be our fate, with French America as an independent republic at last, then the challenges we face will largely be the ones we have ignored or not understood until recently.

We will need to assert our primacy as a hemispheric state, and define a national strategy and a national ideology for the future. And if we don't start doing these things before Québec separates, Canada may require the kind of harsh direction we have not experienced since World War II to ensure our survival.

Yet restructuring Canada without Québec will require more than this: it will require a rebirth of our self-esteem and an end to the demeaning and self-seeking attitude which has been the mark of our decline as a nation in the late 1970s. Separation must see the end of Canada as a "crybaby" nation.

Canada will be neither poor nor totally bereft when Québec goes. We have creativity, a sense of purpose and some basic drives.

Let's not forget our times of greatness: the feat of Confederation, linking the infant nation by rail, great sacrifice in the two world wars, our economic and military role as a middle-sized world power in the 1940s and '50s, the spontaneous burst of patriotism during our Centennial year.

The Canadian identity will have to be for a time a more nationalistic one as we make efforts to keep intact what is left of Confederation.

It is also important that Canada relate to Québec without rancor, even though many English Canadians will probably never understand why separation happened. We will have to negotiate with a republican government on a catalog of thorny crises. A radical restructuring of tariffs, negotiations on the operation of the St. Lawrence Seaway, acquiring a passage across Québec to link Canada and the Maritime region, negotiations for disassembling the crown corporations—all will receive top priority.

And these will have to be conducted by a federal government which is trying to reorganize itself and other institutions at the same time.

When we formed Confederation in 1867, we rejected the Manifest Destiny that sought to plant the U.S. flag from the Isthmus of Panama to the North Pole. Now we will have to reject it again at a time when our intimate industrial, technological and financial associations with the U.S. will make independent survival more difficult than in 1776, 1812 or 1867.

Canada without Québec will need both determination and magnanimity—to survive against American pressures for union, to assure peaceful coexistence with the new Québec nation, and to rebuild a strong national presence in the world community.

NOTES

1. *New York Times*, February 11, 1977.
2. John D. Harbron, "Mind Those PQs," *Barron's*, November 28, 1976, p. 15.
3. "New prices mean another $1 million a year for the oil firms," *Globe and Mail*, June 25, 1977.
4. André Siegfried, *Le Canada: Puissance Internationale* (Paris: Librairie Armand Colin, 1956).
5. João Paulo dos Reis Velloso, *Novas Dimensões da Sociedade Brasileira*, Rio de Janeiro, 1972; and "Amazônia: The New Farming and Ranching Frontier," *Economic Letter*, Banco Real, New York and São Paulo, March 1977, p. 1.
6. Norman A. Bailey and Ronald M. Schneider, "Brazil's Foreign Policy: A Case Study in Upward Mobility," *Inter-American Economic Affairs* 27, no. 4 (Spring 1974), p. 6.
7. From a speech by Richard Rohmer, Mid-Canada Development Corridor Conference, Lakehead University, Thunder Bay, Ontario, August 22, 1969.
8. *Mid-Canada Report*, Mid-Canada Corridor Foundation Inc. (Toronto: 1971).
9. Canadian Press news report, June 15, 1977.
10. For a detailed analysis of the tanker and tug icebreaker concept see "Canadian shipyards face a battle for big LNG contract," *Globe and Mail*, June 9, 1977.
11. Donald H. Thain and Mark C. Baetz, "Canada's Way Ahead. . .On Course or Headed For Disaster?" *Business Quarterly*, School of Business Administration, University of Western Ontario, vol. 42/1, pp. 25-26.
12. Sanford Rose, "Why the Multinational Tide is Ebbing," *Fortune*, August 1977, p. 116.
13. Harry Bruce, "Atlantic Orphans," *Weekend*, April 2, 1977.

Selected Bibliography

(Reference works not cited in chapter notes.)

CANADA

Blishen, Bernard; Jones, Frank E.; Naegele, Kaspar D.; and Porter, John, eds. *Canadian Society: Sociological Perspectives*. Toronto: Macmillan, 1961.

Burpee, Lawrence J., ed. *An Historical Atlas of Canada*. Toronto: Thomas Nelson and Sons, 1927.

Craig, Gerald M. *Upper Canada: The Formative Years (1781-1941)*. Toronto: McClelland and Stewart, Canadian Centenary Series, 1963.

Dafoe, John W. *Canada: An American Nation*. New York: Columbia University Press, 1935.

Easterbrook, W.T., and Aitken, Hugh G. J. *Canadian Economic History*. Toronto: Macmillan, 1958.

Hogan, George. *The Conservative in Canada*. Toronto: McClelland and Stewart, 1963.

Lower, Arthur R.M. *Colony to Nation*. Toronto: Longmans, Green, 1947.

Newman, Peter C. *Renegade in Power: The Diefenbaker Years*. Toronto: McClelland and Stewart, 1963.

Roberts, Leslie. *C.D.: The Life and Times of Clarence Decatur Howe*. Toronto: Clarke, Irwin, 1957.

Rotstein, Abraham. *The Precarious Homestead: Essays on Economics, Technology and Nationalism*. Toronto: New Press, 1973.

Scott, F. R. *Canada Today: A Study of her National Interests and National Policy*. Toronto: Oxford University Press, 1938.

QUÉBEC

Bergeron, Léandre. *Petit manuel d'histoire du Québec*. Montreal: Editions québécoises.

Cook, Ramsay. *Le sphinx parle français: Un canadien-anglais s'interroge sur le problème québécois*. Translated by François Rinfret. Montreal: Editions HMH, Collection Aujourd'hui, 1966.

Desbarats, Peter. *René*. Toronto: McClelland and Stewart, 1976.

Dion, Gerard, and O'Neill, Louis. *Le Chrétien et les élections*. Montreal: Editions de l'homme, 1960.

157

Gaboury, Jean-Pierre. *Le Nationalisme de Lionel Groulx: aspects idéologiques*. Ottawa: Editions de l'Université d'Ottawa, 1970.

Julien, Pierre-André; Lamonde, Pierre; and Latouche, Daniel. *Québec 2001: Une société refroidie*. Montreal: Editions du Boreal Express, 1976.

McDonough, John Thomas. *Charbonneau & Le Chef*. Toronto: McClelland and Stewart, 1968.

Morin, Claude. *Québec Versus Ottawa: The Struggle for Self-Government (1960-1972)*. Toronto: University of Toronto Press, 1976.

Murray, Vera. *Le Parti québécois: de la fondation à la prise du pouvoir*. Collection Science politique. Montreal, Hurtubise HMH, Cahiers du Québec, 1976.

Pelletier, Rejean. *Les militants du R.I.N.* Travaux de recherche en science sociale. Ottawa: Editions de l'Université d'Ottawa, 1974.

Saywell, John. *The Rise of the Parti Québécois, 1967-1976*. Toronto: University of Toronto Press, 1977.

Trudeau, Pierre Elliott. *Le Fédéralisme et la société canadienne-française*. Montreal: Editions HMH, 1967.

Trudel, Marcel. *Histoire de la Nouvelle France*. Montreal: FIDES, 1963.

Wade, Mason. *The French Canadians, 1960-1967*. rev. ed. 2 vols. Toronto: Macmillan, 1968.

LATIN AMERICA

Baklanoff, Eric N. *Expropriation of U.S. Investments in Cuba, Mexico and Chile*. New York and Washington: Praeger Publishers, 1975.

Baklanoff, Eric N., ed. *New Perspectives on Brazil*. Nashville, Tenn.: Vanderbilt University Press, 1966.

Cavers, David F., and Nelson, James R. *Electric Power Regulation in Latin America*. Baltimore, Johns Hopkins Press, 1959.

Fontaine, Roger W., and Theberge, James D., eds. *Latin America's New Internationalism: The End of Hemispheric Isolation*. Praeger Publishers in conjunction with the Center for Strategic and International Studies, Georgetown University, Washington, D.C., 1976.

Hamlin, D.L.B., ed. *The Latin Americas*. Toronto: Canadian Institute on Public Affairs, 1960.

Haring, C.H. *The Spanish Empire in America*. New York: Harcourt, Brace & World, Harbinger Books Edition, 1963.

Herzog, Jésus Silva. *Breve Historia de la Revolución Mexicana* [Short history of the Mexican revolution]. 2 vols. Mexico City and Buenos Aires: Fondo de la Cultura Económica, 1962.

Lipset, Seymour, and Solari, Aldo, eds. *Elites in Latin America*. Toronto: Oxford University Press, 1967.

Mesa-Lago, Carmelo. *Cuba in the 1970s: Pragmatism and Institutionalization*. Albuquerque: University of New Mexico Press, 1974.

Index

161